AHMED V. BUCKNER AND COOPER & STEWART, LLC

Third Edition

Case File
Trial Materials

AHMED V. BUCKNER AND COOPER & STEWART, LLC

Third Edition
Case File
Trial Materials

Formerly Polisi v. Clark and Parker & Gould

Anthony J. Bocchino

Jack E. Feinberg Professor of Litigation, Emeritus
Temple University Beasley School of Law

David A. Sonenshein

Jack E. Feinberg Professor of Law, Emeritus
Temple University Beasley School of Law

Deanne C. Siemer

Managing Director, Wilsie Co. LLC
Washington, D.C.

NITA®

NATIONAL INSTITUTE FOR TRIAL ADVOCACY

Address inquiries to:
Reprint Permission
National Institute for Trial Advocacy
1685 38th Street, Suite 200
Boulder, CO 80301-2735
Phone: (800) 225-6482
Fax: (720) 890-7069
Email: permissions@nita.org

ISBN 978-1-60156-841-0
FBA1841
eISBN 978-1-60156-842-7
FBA1842

Printed in the United States of America

Official co-publisher of NITA.
WKLegaledu.com/NITA

ACKNOWLEDGMENTS

We thank the participants in the inaugural class of Temple Law School's LLM in Trial Advocacy who worked through an earlier version of this file as part of their program and provided insight into improving the realism of the case file. We also are grateful to our Civil Procedure students who utilized another form of this case file and provided helpful suggestions on its improvement.

We are indebted to Jerome Staller, PhD, and Stephanie Thomas, PhD, of the Center for Forensic Economic Studies in Philadelphia, who wrote the expert witness reports that appear in this file.

We are grateful for the professional assistance from Kenneth Frank, CPA, president of the accounting firm of R.A. Mercer & Co., PC. in presenting the accounting aspects of this case file.

The authors recognize the graphic design work donated by Jennica Bocchino, an Art Director at T-Brand, the graphic arts group at the New York Times.

Finally, we are grateful for our editor at NITA, Virginia Judd, whose high professional standards and unfailing good humor contributed to both the quality of the work and the enjoyment we had in completing it. She assisted in making the file more understandable, internally consistent, and absolutely correct regarding the law involved in this casefile.

AJB

DAS

DCS

CONTENTS

INTRODUCTION 1

COMPLAINT 3

ANSWER 9

MATERIALS FOR THE PLAINTIFF 11

    Deposition of Kiya Ahmed 13

    Deposition of Bill Weisman 39

    Statement of Rachel Levin 57

MATERIALS FOR THE DEFENDANTS 61

    Deposition of Paul Buckner 63

    Deposition of Danielle Reddick 77

    Statement of Mary Langford 87

EXPERT REPORTS 93

    Cameron Palmero, PhD, for Defense Counsel 95

    Memo from Associate Re: Palmero 107

    Aki Chau, PhD, for Plaintiff Counsel 109

    Memo from Associate Re: Chau 119

EXHIBITS 121

    Exhibit 1.   Ahmed Resume 123

    Exhibit 2.   Hiring Letter 125

    Exhibit 3. A–G Ahmed Evaluation Forms 127

    Exhibit 4. A–F Ahmed Salary Letters 135

    Exhibit 5. A–H DeAngelo Evaluation 141

    Exhibit 6.   NCW Commendation Letter Re: Ahmed 149

    Exhibit 7. A–B C&S YR-9 Staff Accountants, Group Evaluations, and Billable Hours Records 151

    Exhibit 8.   7/9/YR-2 Phone Log for Paul Buckner 153

    Exhibit 9.   7/15/YR-2 Phone Log for Paul Buckner 155

    Exhibit 10.   Weisman Draft of Buckner Recommendation Letter for Ahmed 157

    Exhibit 11.   Buckner Letter to Randall Re: Ahmed 159

    Exhibit 12.   Buckner Letter to Miller Re: Ahmed 161

    Exhibit 13.   Buckner Letter to Warren Re: Ahmed 163

    Exhibit 14.   EEOC Notice of Charge of Discrimination 165

Exhibit 15.   C&S Response to Exhibit 167

Exhibit 16.   EEOC Right to Sue Letter 169

Exhibit 17.   Buckner Letter to Purcell Re: Ahmed 171

Exhibit 18.   Affidavit of John Randall... 173

JURY INSTRUCTIONS.. **175**

VERDICT FORM **179**

DEDICATION

For Professor Bocchino:

To my sisters and their husbands,
Barbara & Cedric and Carol & Garry

For Ms. Siemer:

To my long-time colleagues in trial advocacy teaching,
Frank Rothschild and Edward Stein

INTRODUCTION

This gender discrimination and defamation case is the new incarnation of the popular case file, *Polisi v. Clark*. The defendant business has been changed from a law firm to an accounting firm. The plaintiff is now a woman of Middle Eastern heritage. The basic fact pattern remains the same.

Kiya Ahmed claims she was denied partnership in the defendant accounting firm, Cooper & Stewart (C&S), because she terminated a sexual relationship with defendant Paul Buckner. She also claims gender discrimination based on a sexual harassment claim against the defendants, as well as a hostile work environment claim against both defendants. The plaintiff further claims that she was denied partnership in C&S based on her religion (Islam) and ethnicity. Finally, she claims that she was defamed by the Defendant Buckner and C&S.

The parties have stipulated that all documents are authentic and meet the requirements of the Original Documents Rule. Other requirements for later admissibility must be established by offering counsel.

This case file is completely fictitious and any resemblance to any person living or dead is coincidental.

All years in these materials are stated in the following form:

1) YR-0 indicates the actual year in which the case is being tried (i.e., the present year);

2) YR-1 indicates the next preceding year (please use the actual year);

3) YR-2 indicates the second preceding year (please use the actual year), etc.

Electronic exhibits can be found at the following website:

http://bit.ly/1P20Jea

Password: Ahmed1

IN THE UNITED STATES
DISTRICT COURT
DISTRICT OF NITA

KIYA AHMED,	)	
Plaintiff,	)	CIVIL ACTION NO. YR-1-4678
	)	
v.	)	JURY TRIAL DEMANDED
	)	
PAUL BUCKNER	)	
and	)	
COOPER & STEWART,	)	
Defendants.	)	

COMPLAINT

Parties

1. Plaintiff, Kiya Ahmed, is a female, Egyptian/American adult individual, who is a citizen of Nita and of the United States and a practicing Muslim. She resides in Nita City, Nita.

2(a). Defendant Cooper & Stewart (C&S) is a professional corporation organized under the laws of the State of Nita, engaged in the provision of professional accounting services in Nita, with its offices at Four Independence Square, Nita City, Nita.

2(b). Defendant C&S is an employer within the meaning of Section 701(b) of Title VII of the Civil Rights Act of 1964, as amended, 42 U.S.C. § 2000e(b), in that it engages in an industry affecting commerce and has had fifteen or more employees for each working day in each of twenty or more calendar weeks in the current or pending calendar year.

3(a). Defendant Paul Buckner is a male, adult individual who is a citizen of Nita and the United States. He resides in Nita City, Nita.

3(b). Defendant Paul Buckner at all times material to this lawsuit, was and continues to be a partner in the Defendant C&S, and an agent of C&S within the meaning of 42 U.S.C. § 2000e(b).

Jurisdiction and Venue

4. Plaintiff invokes this court's jurisdiction pursuant to 28 U.S.C. § 1331, 42 U.S.C. § 2000e-5(f)(3) and invokes Supplemental Jurisdiction pursuant to 28 U.S.C. § 1367. This action arises pursuant to 42 U.S.C. § 2000e et seq., Title VII of the Civil Rights Act of 1964, as amended.

5. All conditions precedent to the filing of this action have been satisfied in that the Equal Employment Opportunity Commission of the United States issued its Right to Sue notice on December 28, YR-2.

6. Venue is appropriate in the District of Nita because the defendants both reside in the State of Nita, the claims arose there, and the defendants may both be served with process there.

CLAIM I

<u>Violation of the Civil Rights Act of 1964—Gender Discrimination</u>

7. Plaintiff completed a graduate program at Nita University Business School with an MBA degree and passed the Nita certified public accounting exam. Plaintiff became a licensed CPA in YR-9. Defendant C&S hired Plaintiff as a senior accountant after Plaintiff became a licensed CPA. Plaintiff worked as a senior accountant for seven years prior to her being forced to resign her position in the firm.

8. In June of YR-3, Defendant Buckner initiated a sexual relationship with Plaintiff while she was an employee of C&S working for and under the supervision of Buckner on the business of the Defendant C&S.

9. In January of YR-2, Plaintiff terminated the sexual relationship with Defendant Buckner.

10. Although Plaintiff received excellent evaluations of her work over the period of her employment with Defendant C&S, Plaintiff was rejected for partnership while male associates who were less qualified than Plaintiff were accepted for partnership with the Defendant C&S in YR-2.

11. Plaintiff was rejected for partnership in the Defendant firm because she terminated a sexual relationship with her supervisor, Defendant Paul Buckner, in violation of Plaintiff's rights under Title VII of the Civil Rights Act of 1964, as amended, 42 U.S.C. § 2000e et seq.

CLAIM II

<u>Violation of the Civil Rights Act of 1964—Quid Pro Quo Sexual Harassment</u>

12. Plaintiff incorporates by reference paragraphs 1 through 11 hereof, all of which amount to quid pro quo sexual harassment in violation of Title VII of the Civil Rights Act of 1964, 42 U.S.C. § 2000e, et seq.

CLAIM III

<u>Violation of the Civil Rights Act of 1964—Hostile Working Environment</u>

13. Plaintiff incorporates by reference paragraph 1 through 12 hereof.

14. Defendant Buckner, while Plaintiff's supervisor, sexually harassed Plaintiff by, on numerous occasions, making unwelcome sexual advances to Plaintiff, culminating in a sexually intimate affair, all of which created and imposed on Plaintiff a sexually hostile and abusive working environment in violation of Plaintiff's rights pursuant to Title VII of the Civil Rights Act of 1964, as amended, 42 U.S.C. § 2000e, et seq.

15. Defendant C&S had a policy that allowed senior members of the firm with control over the advancement of junior professional accountant employees, to have sexual relations with junior accountants, thereby creating a work environment, hostile on its face, to junior members of the firm.

16. Defendant Buckner had numerous sexual relationships with employees of the Defendant C&S, which were specifically allowed, encouraged, and abetted by the Defendant C&S, by lack of any sort of discipline of Defendant Buckner, and the release from employment of C&S of those women with whom Defendant Buckner had a sexual relationship that ended, adding to the hostile work environment of the Defendant C&S.

<u>CLAIM IV—Religious and Ethnic Discrimination</u>

17. Plaintiff incorporates paragraphs 1 through 16 hereof:

18. Plaintiff is Egyptian/American and a practicing Muslim.

19. C&S has an apparent policy against the hiring of Arabs and practicing Muslims.

20. C&S discriminated against Plaintiff based on her ethnicity and religion when she was denied partnership and fired from her position as a professional CPA at C&S.

WHEREFORE, Plaintiff prays that this Court will:

a. Issue a declaratory judgment declaring that the actions of Defendants C&S and Buckner, as set forth in this Complaint, violated Plaintiff's rights under Title VII of the Civil Rights Act of 1964, as amended, 42 U.S.C. § 2000e, et seq.

b. Enjoin and restrain Defendants C&S and Buckner and all other persons acting on behalf of, or in concert with, them from engaging in such unlawful practices.

c. Enter judgment in favor of Plaintiff, and against Defendants C&S and Buckner, for back pay in the amount of wages and fringe benefits it is determined that Plaintiff lost as a result of Defendants' unlawful conduct, together with interest.

d. Enter judgment in favor of Plaintiff and against Defendants C&S and Buckner, reinstating plaintiff to the position she would have had absent Defendants' unlawful conduct. In the alternative, award plaintiff front pay in the amount of wages and benefits it is determined that Plaintiff is likely to lose because of Defendants' unlawful conduct.

e. Enter judgment in favor of Plaintiff, and against Defendants for compensatory damages, including but not limited to, damages for mental anguish and humiliation, together with interest.

f. Award Plaintiff reasonable attorneys' fees together with the costs of this action.

g. Award such other and further legal and equitable relief as may be appropriate to redress fully the deprivation of Plaintiff's rights, to prevent their recurrence in the future and to protect other C&S employees from such unlawful behavior.

CLAIM IV

Defamation

21. Plaintiff incorporates herein by reference paragraphs 1 through 20 hereof.

22. Following Plaintiff's rejection for partnership by the Defendant C&S, Plaintiff applied for CPA positions with other accounting firms.

23. When Defendant C&S was asked by at least two of the above-mentioned prospective employers for its opinion regarding Plaintiff's personality and abilities, Defendant Buckner maliciously responded with false and slanderous statements which defamed Plaintiff regarding her personal and professional reputation.

24. The false statements made by Defendant Buckner were made with the express, implied, or apparent authority of Defendant C&S, and Defendant C&S ratified those statements by not repudiating them.

25. As a result of the false and slanderous statements maliciously made by Defendant Buckner, and ratified by Defendant C&S, Plaintiff has suffered substantial emotional distress, mental anguish and pain and suffering; as well as damage to her personal and professional reputation and earning capacity.

WHEREFORE, Plaintiff demands judgment against Defendants, Cooper & Stewart and Buckner, for compensatory damages in an amount in excess of $1,000,000.

JURY DEMAND

Plaintiff demands a jury trial for all claims triable by a jury.

Respectfully submitted,

David Darrow, Esquire
1500 Main Street
Nita City, Nita 10076
Dated: February 2, YR-1.

VERIFICATION

I, Kiya Ahmed, am the plaintiff in the above-captioned action. I have read this complaint and verify that the allegations in it are true.

Kiya Ahmed

Signed and sworn before me in the County of Nita this 2nd day of February, YR-0.

Notary Public

IN THE UNITED STATES
DISTRICT COURT
FOR THE DISTRICT OF NITA

KIYA AHMED,　　　　　　　　　　　)
Plaintiff,　　　　　　　　　　　　　)　　　　　CIVIL ACTION NO. YR-1-4678
　　　　　　　　　　　　　　　　　　)
v.　　　　　　　　　　　　　　　　　)　　　　　JURY TRIAL DEMANDED
　　　　　　　　　　　　　　　　　　)
PAUL BUCKNER　　　　　　　　　　)
and　　　　　　　　　　　　　　　　)
COOPER & STEWART,　　　　　　　　)
Defendants.　　　　　　　　　　　　)

ANSWER OF DEFENDANTS PAUL BUCKNER AND COOPER & STEWART

By way of answer, Defendants, Paul Buckner and Cooper & Stewart, respond to Plaintiff's allegations as follows:

1. Admit.

2(a). Admit.

2(b). Admit.

3(a). Admit.

3(b). Admit.

4. Admit.

5. Admit.

6. Admit.

7. Admit the Defendant accounting firm hired Plaintiff as an accountant in YR-9 and that Plaintiff worked at the firm for seven years before resigning her position.

8. Deny that the Defendant Buckner initiated the relationship. The relationship was mutually, freely, and willingly entered into by Plaintiff and the Defendant Buckner.

9. Admit.

10. Admit that Plaintiff was rejected for partnership, but deny that Plaintiff received excellent evaluations over the period of her employment with the Defendant accounting firm.

11. Deny.

12. Deny.

13. Paragraph 13 contains no statement of fact to admit or deny.

14. Deny.

15. Deny all allegations incorporated by reference which were heretofore denied and admit those allegations already admitted. Deny the allegation of quid pro quo sexual harassment.

16. Deny all allegations incorporated by reference which were heretofore denied and admit those allegations already admitted.

17. Paragraph 17 contains no statement of fact to admit or deny.

18. Admit.

19. Deny.

20. Deny.

21. Paragraph 21 contains no statement of fact to admit or deny.

22. Defendants have insufficient knowledge to admit or deny.

23. Deny.

24. Deny.

25. Deny.

For the Defendants,
Paul Buckner and Cooper & Stewart,

Jane Jackson

Jane Jackson, Esq.

Materials for the Plaintiff

DEPOSITION OF KIYA AHMED

1   My name is Kiya Ahmed. I am an American-born child of my citizen parents, who im-
2   migrated from Egypt in YR-45. We are practicing Muslims. I live at 7010 Greenhill Rd. in
3   Nita City. I am forty-one years old and the single parent of two children: David, who is
4   twenty-one and a senior at Nita University, and Mina, who is nineteen and a sophomore
5   at Conwell College in the northwest part of the state. Until December 15th of YR-2, I was
6   an accountant with the firm of Cooper & Stewart in Nita City, at which time I was forced
7   out of the firm. Since then I have accepted a position as a Practice Professor of Law and
8   Accounting at Nita University School of Law, where I teach Accounting for Lawyers, Basic
9   Issues in Forensic Accounting, and a seminar in Forensic Accounting in Anti-Trust Litiga-
10   tion. I began this position as a Practice Professor, which is a Presidential (non-tenure
11   track) position, although I hope to join the tenure track faculty within the next five years
12   as I build my scholarly bona fides. During the spring semester, YR-1, I was an Adjunct Pro-
13   fessor at the Law School. I was hired as a full-time member of the faculty on a three-year,
14   renewable contract in YR-1.

15

16   I was born and raised in Wallingford, Connecticut, where I attended the public schools. In
17   YR-23 I graduated from Lyman Hall High School and enrolled at the University of Pennsylva-
18   nia in Philadelphia, where I majored in business at the Wharton School. I also had a minor
19   concentration in accounting. During my freshman year I met Gregory Meyers, who was an
20   MBA student at the Wharton School at Penn. We dated very seriously and in the spring of
21   my freshman year, I became pregnant with my son, David. Greg and I married that summer,
22   and he took a job with the Nita Fidelity Bank in their foreign investment division. I trans-
23   ferred from Penn to the University of Nita, where I continued my studies.

24

25   My daughter, Mina, was born in YR-19, one month after I graduated from Nita University
26   Business School with a BS degree in business and a minor in accounting. I was a good stu-
27   dent. I graduated summa cum laude and was elected to Phi Beta Kappa. Greg and I decided
28   that it would be best for the kids if I stayed home with them while they were little, so I put
29   my career on hold. Unfortunately, Greg and I were not meant to be married to each other.
30   His trips to Europe became longer and longer; after a while, I didn't even mind. In YR-17,
31   we divorced, and Greg moved to Europe to work for an investment house there. I needed
32   to work to help support my kids, but also to keep my sanity.

33

34   Relying on my undergraduate minor in accounting, I applied to several accounting firms
35   for positions performing routine accounting services—the kind that did not require hand-
36   ling by the CPAs who were on a professional track at the firm. I received several offers and
37   chose to go with Cooper & Stewart. I liked the flexibility C&S offered; it gave me time to
38   care for my kids when that was needed. They were also willing to assign me to engage-
39   ments that did not take me out of town for more than a night or two. They understood
40   that I was a single mother and that to send me out of town was a hardship. No other firm
41   was willing to give me such assurances, so I went with C&S. I started work there in late
42   YR-16.

1   C&S is a relatively large accounting firm that provides the full range of professional audit and
2   tax advice in a four-state area that includes Nita, although there are several partners in the
3   audit and tax sections whose practice is national in scope. The firm now has approximately
4   sixty professionals, of whom twenty-six are partners. At the time I went to work for C&S as
5   a staff assistant, it was one of the largest accounting firms in Nita City, but only had about
6   sixteen partners. I was assigned to the audit section of the firm, which is the most presti-
7   gious; it also performs expert witness/litigation support services in complicated civil litiga-
8   tion. The firm has a tax section that also does estate planning work, and a small business
9   section that performs the full range of accounting services for small businesses including
10   uncomplicated, straightforward litigation support engagements like in personal injury cases.
11

12   I worked for quite a few of the partners at the firm, but in YR-15 I was assigned to work on
13   a large commercial case involving several of the biggest banks in Nita City. The partner in
14   charge of that engagement was a rising star at the firm, Paul Buckner, and I worked very
15   closely with him and with Bill Weisman (who at the time was a relatively new partner
16   at the firm) for about two years. When the case came to trial, in January of YR-13, I was
17   selected to be part of the accounting team providing financial analysis for the law firm
18   representing the main defendant in the case. Paul was apparently pleased with my work
19   because I received a substantial bonus and a pay raise when our client settled the case on
20   very favorable terms, and several of the banks became clients of the firm for all their audit
21   and forensic accounting matters.
22

23   Paul Buckner has always had a reputation in the firm as a womanizer. Several senior staff
24   accountants warned me to watch out for him when I joined the firm, as did some of the
25   women staff assistants. They said Paul was in a very unhappy marriage and that he had
26   used this fact as an entree with women in the office, including clerical people, staff assis-
27   tants, staff accountants, and even senior accountants. Apparently, he had promised a few
28   young women that he would leave his wife to be with them, but that never happened. In
29   the end, the women would either quit the firm or be fired, and Paul would go on to his
30   next conquest.
31

32   During the bank case in YR-15 through YR-13, I worked very closely with Paul for long hours
33   and in close quarters, and he never really came on to me. There was some innocent flirting
34   on his part, but maybe because of his reputation, or maybe because he reminded me of
35   my husband, I steered clear of him. I don't know if he was interested in a personal relation-
36   ship with me at the time, but as I said, I never really responded to his flirting, and he never
37   made any inappropriate advances other than from time to time, when talking with me, he
38   would touch me. Things like, when he was reading something over my shoulder, he would
39   put his hands on my shoulders. Although this bothered me, I never said anything; after all,
40   he was the boss and even though I was uncomfortable with the physical contact, it did not
41   seem to be overtly sexual in nature.
42

43   Sometime later I learned Paul was involved with a woman CPA at the firm, who was also
44   working on the engagement. Her name is Susan McGinty. Susan left the firm sometime

1   after the bank case. She is now a partner in a mid-sized accounting firm in Philadelphia.
2   The rumor was that when Paul refused to leave his wife, Susan put her foot down, and as
3   a result she was forced to leave the firm.
4
5   During the bank engagement, Paul frequently complimented my work. He often said things
6   to the effect that I was the equal of many of the young CPAs who were working on the
7   project. Once he even kidded Bill Weisman in front of me, saying one day I was going to
8   take Bill's place. In fact, both Paul Buckner and Bill encouraged me to get an MBA and sit for
9   the CPA examinations. The accounting profession has strict rules about credentials. First,
10 you must attend an accredited college or university full time for five years and take the
11 required accounting course credit hours. You can take them either as an undergraduate or
12 during an MBA program at a university level. Then you must take a four-part CPA exam and
13 pass all the parts within one year. You can take parts over again if you don't get a passing
14 grade, but you must pass all of them within a twelve-month period. Also, either before or
15 after the exam, you are required to complete a one-year internship working on accounting
16 matters with an accounting firm.
17
18 Paul recommended I leave the firm and go to school full time but, by that time, my ex-
19 husband's child support payments were sporadic at best, and it was an economic necessity
20 for me to continue to work. I applied to, and was accepted for, an online program at Nita
21 University School of Business in the MBA program and began classes in the fall of YR-13.
22 Both Paul and Bill (who was a graduate of Nita University School of Business) wrote letters
23 of recommendation for me. I'm sure they were helpful because my application was a little
24 late but I still was accepted. The online programs have grown in popularity and quality over
25 the years given the realities of older students with economic responsibilities who need to
26 work while attending school. It is the position of many business schools, especially Nita
27 University's, that the courses are the same, the professors the same, and the academic
28 rigor equal in both the full-time and online programs. At any rate, it wasn't a choice for
29 me, given my single-parent status.
30
31 I continued to work at C&S during my years in the MBA program. The firm was very good
32 about accommodating my school schedule; they allowed me to take some time off dur-
33 ing exams and make it up later. I also had permission to use the firm's resources for my
34 research and business and accounting simulation projects during non-work hours. During
35 the entire time I was in the MBA program, Paul Buckner expressed enthusiasm for me
36 and my career. When I made Dean's list in my first semester of business school, he con-
37 gratulated me and offered to take me out to dinner to celebrate. Because I was so busy—
38 between work, school, and my kids—I turned him down for dinner; but did agree to go to
39 lunch. At lunch he was very charming and acted genuinely interested in me, my kids, and
40 my career. He said I should be sure to make some time for myself. That may have been
41 great advice, but the time just wasn't there.
42
43 Paul's interest in my career continued throughout my MBA program. He was always avail-
44 able to discuss a problem I had with my school work or with an engagement I was working

1   on at the firm. Although his habit of touching my arm or shoulder when we talked embar-
2   rassed me, I never said anything to him because the touching, although unwanted, was
3   not, as I said earlier, overtly sexual. He was the same with both men and women, so I just
4   assumed he was a handsy person, but I didn't like it at all. It turned out, with me and other
5   women, to be his first step in pursuing a sexual relationship.
6
7   After I achieved top 5 percent grades in my first year in the MBA program, Bill suggested
8   I apply for an accounting internship with the firm; I would get a raise, and a year of internship
9   is required to get a CPA license. I was surprised because C&S doesn't have a large internship
10 program—maybe one or two every few years. The interns leave too often, and they don't
11 want to invest the resources. I also knew C&S never hired its interns, but I didn't think there
12 was any chance I would get a job offer from them at all, so I applied and got the position.
13
14 The work I did as an accounting intern in the beginning was not much different than my
15 earlier work at the firm as a staff assistant, because people were used to seeing me around
16 as a staff assistant. I complained to Bill about this, and he went to bat for me with Paul.
17 With their help, I was repeatedly assigned to the support team when Paul Buckner was
18 hired as an expert witness, when that occurred in Nita or the Nita area—again, I needed
19 to stay close to my children. As I became more sophisticated in our work on expert witness
20 engagements, so did my assignments. Although I did not receive formal evaluations in that
21 position at C&S, I was rehired each year, and my pay was increased on a regular basis.
22
23 In addition, unlike most of the accounting interns (who are usually undergraduate or grad-
24 uate students in accounting and do not have a CPA degree or license), I received bonuses
25 each year. To tell you the truth, I was quite surprised when I received a bonus at the end
26 of my first year as an accounting intern because I knew the interns normally did not get
27 bonuses. Paul Buckner personally gave me that bonus check. I had just finished roof repairs
28 on my small house, and I feared we were looking at a lean Christmas when he gave me the
29 check. The bonus was something like $2,000, and it could not have come at a better time.
30 I was so excited I gave Paul a big hug. I remember he made some comment like, "with that
31 reaction, I wish we could have given you more." What he said embarrassed me, but I re-
32 ally didn't think much of it the time. I just let go of him and thanked him. He told me he
33 had gone to bat for me on the bonus and I was the only accounting intern to receive one.
34 I thanked him again, and that was that.
35
36 I did very well in the MBA program. Even though I had to limit myself to part-time hours,
37 I attended year-round and always made Dean's list. My grades were always in the top
38 5 percent, which was the highest percentile reported. Two of my professors selected me
39 for research work on publications they were writing. I had an acknowledgment note for
40 this work published in my second year and another acknowledgment note published in my
41 third year.
42
43 During the three years of the MBA program, I worked several assignments on Paul Buck-
44 ner's engagements. He always seemed to be pleased with my work. He asked me out to

1 dinner on several occasions, either to celebrate some success of mine at school or the suc-
2 cess of an engagement we worked on together. I always declined because of my schedule,
3 but we did go out to lunch several times. Paul flirted with me, telling me how attractive
4 I was or making comments like "if I weren't a married man, I'd be camped out at your
5 doorstep," and "if I were only ten years younger, I'd fly away with you to a desert island."
6 Although it made me uncomfortable, I made a little joke that he was watching too many
7 1950s movies or ignored him. Since I didn't think he meant anything by the comments,
8 I thought protesting would look silly, and he might view me as an "hysterical woman."
9
10 I know that sounds weak in light of the "Me Too" movement, but he wasn't sexually as-
11 saulting me or doing any harm, other than making me a bit uncomfortable. There wasn't
12 the kind of awareness there is now. Given my life experiences, I thought a bit of discomfort
13 was just part of being an adult in the real world—and my work was by far not the most
14 important thing in my world. I never dwelled on his comments afterward, and they never
15 caused me enough discomfort that I felt I should complain about it.
16
17 During the three years I was working on my MBA degree, Paul Buckner's stock rose steadily
18 with the firm. He was in great demand by trial lawyers for his expert analysis and testi-
19 mony; his engagements became national in scope. He was very well regarded profession-
20 ally within the firm. Everyone in the firm knew Paul was responsible for attracting and
21 keeping some of the firm's best clients—companies with frequent audit matters, including
22 litigation involving complicated audit issues. Because they liked Paul, they brought their
23 regular audit and some business planning business to the firm. His talent and success prob-
24 ably contributed to the firm tolerating his extramarital affairs with coworkers. I can't under-
25 stand why the firm put up with his behavior, but it did. Maybe the firm didn't care about
26 his personal life, so long as he continued to succeed as a partner. In fact, firm policy per-
27 mitted consensual sexual relationships among adult employees. Firm policy also forbade
28 a hostile work environment. Looking back, it's clear both policies can't exist at the same
29 time, but I didn't pay attention because I was not personally involved. I'm embarrassed to
30 say I never spoke up about these policies nor came to the aid of their victims. At any rate,
31 the rumors of his philandering never ceased, and Paul went through several public affairs
32 within the firm while I was getting my MBA degree.
33
34 I know he had a six-month relationship with Ellen Dorsen, who was a senior accountant
35 with the firm. This was in YR-12. She spoke openly of her weekends with Paul and the
36 places they went together. When the affair ended, Ellen took it badly. A few the other ac-
37 countants were very hard on her, given the way she flaunted her relationship with Paul,
38 and it affected her work. The firm eventually fired her. I also know Paul had affairs with two
39 other women who were both staff CPAs with the firm, Karen Newman in YR-11, and Carol
40 Merritt in YR-10. I know this because they were assigned to work on two different engage-
41 ments with Paul, and I worked on both as well.
42
43 Karen was a third-year staff accountant in her late twenties when she had her fling with
44 Paul. When the affair ended after about a month, she confided in me about it. She said Paul

1   had made some statements about leaving his wife, but Karen knew he was lying so she
2   ended the relationship. She initially took the whole thing in stride, but over the next sev-
3   eral months Karen complained to me—and anyone else who would listen—that her work
4   assignments had gotten bad. Rather than being assigned to the high-profile commercial
5   engagements, as she had been in the recent past, she was given work on simple small busi-
6   ness engagements. The firm takes these engagements looking to develop relationships on
7   the "ground floor" with growing businesses—it's a bit of a gamble but pays off if the busi-
8   ness thrives. Still, these assignments went to junior staff, and Karen was way past that level
9   in the firm. She also complained she was having a hard time keeping her billable hours up
10   because she wasn't getting assigned enough work. One of the people she complained to
11   was Bill Weisman, who by that time was a well-respected young partner at the firm and
12   was known to be Paul Buckner's protégé.
13
14   Karen held on for about six months, then left for a job with another firm. She told me
15   dumping Paul was the reason for her bad assignments or lack of assignments; she decided
16   to leave the firm before "they" could damage her reputation. At the time I thought she
17   was overreacting but, given what happened to me, my guess is she did the right thing for
18   herself. I have seen Karen occasionally since she left the firm. When this whole thing hap-
19   pened to me, she somehow heard about it and asked me to lunch. She commiserated with
20   me, saying Paul appeared to be up to his old tricks. Although she didn't name names, she
21   told me there were lots of women, staff accountants or CPAs in the city, who had been
22   forced out of C&S after a relationship with Paul Buckner.
23
24   Carol Merritt's situation was more complicated. At the time she started her affair with
25   Paul, she was a fourth-year staff accountant, about thirty years old, and married. She fell
26   head over heels in love with Paul while working on a case with him. Their affair lasted a
27   good six months. About three months into the affair, she got so serious that she left her
28   husband. I talked to her about Paul before she left her husband and warned her about
29   Paul's reputation. I even suggested she contact Karen Newman or talk to Bill Weisman. She
30   assured me Paul was going to leave his wife and marry her; he was just waiting for the right
31   time, but it would be soon. Of course, Paul never left his wife and, when the case they were
32   working on together ended, he terminated his relationship with Carol about a month later.
33   Carol ended up taking about a month off and came back to the firm only long enough to
34   pack up her office and move out. Rachel Levin—then Charles Milton's administrative assis-
35   tant—told me she was leaving. Rachel and I were friendly at the time, and I talked to Carol
36   at Rachel's suggestion. Carol thanked me for trying to be a good friend when I warned her
37   about Paul. She also told me her husband had taken her back and the two of them were
38   moving to Washington, DC. She said even though Paul had been a jerk, he had given her a
39   great recommendation, and she was going to work for a good firm in DC.
40
41   I think Carol's and Karen's experiences were consistent with Paul Buckner's normal be-
42   havior. He isn't an evil man, but he does evil things. His fatal flaw is he cannot be satisfied
43   with one woman—or at least not for long. But when he's done with them, or they're done
44   with him, he doesn't want them around. I don't know whether he knows or cares how

1   devastating his actions can be. These are hard lessons from my relationship with Paul,
2   and I certainly didn't grasp these things about him back then. While I was working on my
3   MBA degree, I viewed Paul and his affairs as just a fact of life. I had some sympathy for the
4   women who got involved with him, but they were adults and they knew his reputation, so
5   what happened to them seemed to be something they should have suspected. Time has
6   taught me different lessons.
7
8   For me, except for the mild flirtations and the unwanted but relatively innocuous touching,
9   Paul Buckner was a hero. He was one of the best CPAs in the firm, especially for his age.
10 During the time I was working on my MBA degree, Paul was in his late thirties and early
11 forties. I read his expert reports and saw him testify and he was a master at both. He was
12 brilliant. He could explain the most complicated concepts as if they were simple. He also
13 took the time to congratulate me on my successes in my MBA program and to give me a
14 "well done" on the work I did for him and helpful explanations when my work wasn't its
15 best. And although this now seems so inconsistent with his treatment of women, he orga-
16 nized the accountants in the firm to provide free tax advice to poor or middle-class people,
17 especially for a group composed of single mothers. To say I admired him is an understate-
18 ment. He was my role model and mentor. After all, Paul encouraged me to get my MBA
19 degree in order to complete the CPA course requirements. In fact, Paul and Bill Weisman,
20 for whom I did quite a bit of work, are most responsible for my becoming a licensed CPA.
21
22 Like most states, Nita requires CPA exam candidates to complete a one-year internship
23 with an accounting firm. As of YR-9, C&S had never sponsored a CPA exam candidate who
24 qualified through the online MBA program of Nita University School of Business. The firm
25 had hired Nita University graduates, like Bill Weisman, but no one from the online pro-
26 gram. Virtually every CPA license candidate at the firm graduated from one of the "best"
27 university accounting programs from around the country. I was surprised when Paul Buck-
28 ner and Bill Weisman came by my office one day, early in the fall of my third and final year
29 of my MBA program, and invited me to lunch to "talk about my future with the firm." Bill
30 had recently been made a partner. He was considered a rising star and the protégé of Paul
31 Buckner. He was a very active member of the hiring committee. Paul chaired the hiring
32 committee.
33
34 At lunch, they congratulated me on completing the academic course work required for a
35 CPA license. They pointed out that my work at C&S's sponsorship qualified as the intern-
36 ship year required to become a certified CPA. I said I would apply to take the CPA exam
37 right away—which I did, passing all four parts on the first try.
38
39 At lunch, Paul and Bill asked why I had not applied for a CPA position at the firm. I said,
40 "Isn't it obvious? C&S never hires CPAs out of the online program of any university, and they
41 never hire their interns. That's two strikes against me; it's pointless." They both said they
42 were very impressed with my work; it was the equivalent of any of the applicants in the
43 past. Though it wasn't a foregone conclusion I would be hired, they thought I should apply;
44 they would both enthusiastically support my application. To say I was flattered would be

1   an understatement. I had always harbored a fantasy I'd somehow get to be an accountant
2   at C&S, but I never expected it could happen.
3
4   Paul and Bill asked where else I had applied, and I told them the names of the firms. Be-
5   cause of bias against online program graduates in some of the largest firms (including
6   C&S), I had applied to the second tier of firms in the city. They were very good accounting
7   firms but did not have the size, clout, or regional reach of the top firms like C&S. I followed
8   through on my interviews with those firms and, given C&S's interest, even applied to some
9   of the other large firms in the city, several of which offered me interviews.
10
11   Of course, I followed through on Paul and Bill's suggestion and applied to C&S. Although I was
12   nervous, I did well at the preliminary interview and was invited to an interview with the en-
13   tire hiring committee. That interview went even better. The only partner who seemed nega-
14   tive towards me was one of the few women partners in the firm, Danielle Reddick. Danielle
15   was a relatively new partner at the time, and she was trying to develop the small business
16   section within the firm. The idea behind the small business section (as I mentioned before)
17   was that the firm could do work for new and developing businesses on all aspects of account-
18   ing work—from tax/business planning, auditing, and litigation support—at lower rates and
19   for easier tasks on less complicated matters, with the expectation that at least some of these
20   firms would become larger, more profitable, and have more lucrative audit and tax engage-
21   ments available for which the firm would be hired. Danielle also thought the small business
22   section of the firm could handle litigation support engagements on cases not serious enough
23   for the audit section rates, including personal injury damage testimony. At that point she was
24   the only partner focusing on small business work. She had three people working for her, two
25   of whom were women and one an African American man. One was a staff assistant, another
26   was a staff accountant, which is a position held by someone who has passed the CPA exam but
27   does not yet have a CPA license, and a third was a senior accountant who held a CPA license.
28
29   I told the committee I was most interested in commercial audit work, including assignments
30   involving expert accounting testimony, but I still needed to be assigned to work on engage-
31   ments primarily based in Nita City, because of my children. At the time David was twelve
32   and Mina was ten (going on thirty-five) and they needed a lot of my attention. Ms. Reddick
33   reacted negatively in response to my request for Nita-based engagements (as opposed to
34   being sent across country for months at a time). She implied that it was inappropriate for
35   me to ask for special consideration in assignments—and although it might have been, it
36   would have been pointless for me to accept a job that would take me away from my kids for
37   extended periods, because that would have been impossible. I wanted to be upfront about
38   the job flexibility I needed. Prior to my interviews, I wondered how the committee would
39   react, so I ran my problem by Bill Weisman. Bill later told me he had talked it over with Paul
40   Buckner and Paul didn't see a problem. After all, the firm had always accommodated me in
41   my work as a staff assistant, and eventually the kids would be out on their own.
42
43   C&S was the most receptive to my needs of all the accounting firms from whom I received
44   offers, Danielle Reddick notwithstanding. Even though I received offers from five other

1   firms, including one other silk-stocking firm, I went with C&S, partially because of their
2   flexibility, but mostly because I considered their offer an honor. On the day I accepted
3   C&S's offer of the accountant position, Paul Buckner came by my office. He gave me a big
4   hug and welcomed me aboard. I thought it was inappropriate, and he made me a little un-
5   comfortable, but I was so happy to be hired by C&S that I just thanked Paul for all the help
6   he had given me. He told me he'd be sure to ask for me on some of his engagements so we
7   could work closely together. To be honest, I was flattered.
8

9   I graduated in YR-9 from the online MBA program and received several academic awards
10   and prizes at graduation. I am providing you with a copy of my resume, which contains
11   those awards. I graduated summa cum laude and ranked first in the online program class.
12   (See Exhibit 1.) I am proud to say I passed all four parts of the CPA exam—audit, tax, busi-
13   ness law, and accounting—on my first attempt, the summer after I finished my MBA de-
14   gree. The firm gave me six weeks paid salary to study for the exam, as they did with all
15   candidates for CPA licensing. Many did not pass the test on the first try and were precluded
16   from doing any kind of work, predominantly audits, that required a CPA license.
17

18   I received my official letter of appointment from C&S to the accountant position in July of
19   YR-9. (See Exhibit 2.) The general language about my job duties concerned me because
20   there was no mention of my understanding that I would not be assigned to engagements
21   that would take me out of Nita City for extended periods of time. I mentioned this to Bill
22   Weisman, and he told me not to be concerned, the letter was just a form letter and the
23   firm understood my need to be near my children.
24

25   Because the firm sponsored me for the required internship year based on my prior work
26   at the firm, I was able to apply for the state CPA license right away after passing the exam
27   in September YR-9. As soon as I got my license, I was assigned to the audit section, which
28   was my preference. My beginning salary was $85,000. Partially because of my years of
29   experience with the firm—and partially because, as I now realize, I have some talent—
30   I progressed a little faster than some of the other employees at my level in the firm. I think
31   it helped that I was older and had done an MBA program while working full time and hav-
32   ing the responsibility of being a single parent. Because of my maturity, the stress of the job
33   affected me less than it did some of the others at my level.
34

35   To be honest, my workload at C&S as a licensed staff accountant felt less onerous than
36   my workload as a staff assistant and an MBA program student. I was comfortable with
37   the working environment at C&S and knew all the little administrative things you need to
38   know to survive, so I spent a lot less time spinning my wheels. Tracking hours was new for
39   my colleagues, most of whom had come straight from the usual five-year undergraduate
40   CPA degree programs and were twenty-three or twenty-four years old, but I was already
41   familiar with it and it presented no obstacle to my doing my best work.
42

43   I was assigned a wide variety of commercial audit matters and worked with several part-
44   ners. I did very little work with Paul Buckner during my first five years as a CPA at C&S.

1   I occasionally drafted an audit report or a section of an expert report, but I never worked
2   a complete engagement from start to finish with him. That may have been just happen-
3   stance, but it may also have been because of my desire to not become involved in engage-
4   ments that involved a lot of travel for extended periods. C&S has a four-state practice,
5   and Paul was the best auditing expert witness accountant in the firm, which was reflected
6   in the national scope of his practice. He worked hand-in-hand with lawyers, especially in
7   commercial cases, explaining to them the operations of business accounting, the regula-
8   tory recordkeeping requirements and such, so their legal theory reflected the account-
9   ing facts. He was always handling the most important commercial engagements for the
10   firm. When those engagements involved litigation, he and his support team would spend
11   months at a time in the region where the case took place, interviewing witnesses and as-
12   sisting lawyers in preparing for and taking depositions, managing discovery relevant to his
13   analysis, and assisting in making and responding to motions. In addition to the enormous
14   litigation preparation if the case went to trial, Paul was there to advise and testify. As a re-
15   sult, he was frequently out of the office for extended periods of time, so the opportunities
16   to work for him were limited.
17
18   When I did work for Paul, our working relationship was good and, except for an occasional
19   comment about how I looked, he was very professional. In fact, the rumors about Paul and
20   his firm romances were less frequent. I don't know of any affair he had during the period
21   of YR-9 through YR-3. I know Paul's son was almost killed in a car accident in YR-9 and had
22   a long recovery. Maybe that caused him to focus on his family life; I don't know. Whenever
23   I was assigned to one of Paul's engagements, he was always complimentary of my work.
24
25   The partner I did the most work for at C&S during the period of YR-9 through YR-4 was Bill
26   Weisman. In the beginning, Bill requested I work with him on some of his smaller audit en-
27   gagements. While some of my fellow accountants preferred the big engagements because
28   the firm attached more importance to them, I was interested in working on engagements
29   where I could actually get experience providing audit advice, in addition to audit services.
30   By working with Bill on smaller engagements, where there were fewer professionals as-
31   signed, I was involved in virtually all aspects of the engagement. I developed an excellent
32   working relationship with Bill, and, because he had confidence in my abilities, he gave me
33   more responsibility than many of my professional colleagues were getting in their work.
34
35   Bill made sure I got experience advising clients and drafting audit reports. If an engage-
36   ment involved litigation, and Bill was the expert witness, I worked on advising the lawyers
37   on deposition and trial matters. If testimony was required, Bill provided the expert testi-
38   mony and I would assist in his preparation with the lawyers involved.
39
40   Bill also made certain I worked on some of the more prestigious matters in the firm, for
41   political purposes. He counseled me to become known for doing good work on big en-
42   gagements to progress in the firm. In terms of firm politics, big engagements for big cli-
43   ents had the most currency, and so a job well done in one of those engagements did much
44   more for your reputation in the firm than an equally good job on a lesser engagement

1 (involving less money or for a less important client). This is the sort of thing that, but for
2 the guidance of Bill Weisman, I never would have appreciated. When one of the larger
3 firm engagements occurred in Nita City or nearby, Bill would push for me to be on the
4 team for that engagement.
5
6 Bill also counseled me to avoid getting involved in the small business engagements
7 Danielle and her group handled. Ms. Reddick had built a thriving practice within the firm.
8 By YR-4, she had one other partner, a manager, and two staff accountants who worked
9 primarily with her in her engagements. From time to time she needed extra help com-
10 pleting last-minute audit work or providing analysis of a business problem and would ask
11 for volunteers among the professional staff to help. Because I was marginally interested
12 in the work and because Ms. Reddick was one of only four women partners in the firm
13 during my early years with the firm, I did volunteer from time to time to do some work
14 for her. She was very demanding, but I found her comments on my performance fair and
15 helpful. Bill warned me my stock in the firm would be lessened if I became too identified
16 with that practice. Because he was such a good friend and mentor, I followed his advice
17 and never did a major assignment for her. On one occasion, in YR-3, Ms. Reddick asked
18 me to do some work on one of her complicated, small business engagements, involving
19 the equitable distribution of several family interests, but because I was extremely busy
20 on another engagement with tight deadlines, I was unable to accept the assignment and
21 it was given to another accountant. I know Ms. Reddick was offended by my not accept-
22 ing the assignment, but it really was out of my control.
23
24 Once I became a CPA, my performance became subject to the formal review system.
25 During the period of YR-9 through YR-5, as in every year at C&S, my job performance
26 was evaluated annually. As I understood the process, the chair and the deputy chair of
27 the audit section solicited comments from all the partners for whom I worked during the
28 year. Charles Milton was chair of the audit section then, and his deputy was Ted Potter,
29 both of whom I had worked with over the years. I then met with them, close in time to
30 my anniversary date with the firm, which in my case was September. They reviewed my
31 progress with the firm during that meeting and gave me a numerical evaluation. The
32 scale was 1 to 5. I was never given a written evaluation; Mr. Milton and Mr. Potter con-
33 veyed what I assumed was a compilation of the comments made about me and told how
34 the firm would like to see me improve in the upcoming year. These comments appeared
35 to be coming from a file with my name on it. You have shown me some screen shots that
36 refer to my evaluations and, although I have no way of remembering if they track what
37 was said to me in my evaluations, they certainly could. They are accurate concerning
38 my billable hours for each year. (See Exhibits 3A–3G.) They told me the number of other
39 accountants with my status who received the same evaluation as me, or higher. I also
40 learned what my raise would be for the next year. The raise was pegged to the evalua-
41 tion you received. An evaluation of 1 got you a 7 percent raise, a 2 got 5 percent, and a
42 3 got 3 percent. I don't know if there was any raise associated with a 4 because I never
43 got one. I was never given anything in writing during any of my evaluations except a writ-
44 ten confirmation of my raise. (See Exhibits 4A–4F.)

1   In my first evaluation as a CPA, in YR-8, I received an evaluation of 3 and was told that,
2   within my cohort of fifteen staff accountants, two received the evaluation of 2 and eight
3   received the evaluation of 3. The remainder received 4. I never had received a grade in
4   school lower than a B, so I was a little taken aback. Mr. Milton explained that the partners
5   for whom I worked were generally happy with my work, but I needed to work on being
6   more concise in my writing style. He also said my billable hours were okay, but others billed
7   more hours, and my recovery rate (the amount of charges for hours worked clients actually
8   paid) was a little lower than the 80 percent expected. Bill Weisman approached me later
9   and assured me my work was just fine; if I just kept plugging away, I would be all right.
10
11 I was determined to improve, and I did. In YR-7 through YR-5, I was evaluated as a 2. In
12 YR-7, there were three others in my group of professionals with the evaluation of 2; in
13 YR- 6, three other 2's; and in YR-5, four other professionals were evaluated as high as a 2.
14 There were no 1's given to any of the staff accountants in the audit practice during these
15 four years but, as I understand it, that was not unusual. I guess they just wanted to keep
16 us working. There must have been some low evaluations however, because by YR-5, the
17 group of non-partner professionals was dwindling. Eight of the original fifteen remained.
18 Some people had gone on to other firms, either within Nita City or in other states. One
19 person, Gary Sherman, who was considered one of the brightest and most talented staff
20 accountants, took a teaching position at the University of Conwell Business School in the
21 northwest part of the state. And two people who were interested in getting some expert
22 witness testifying experience had taken positions as staff accountants in two different
23 sections with the U.S. Department of Justice.
24
25 Each of my oral evaluations in YR-7 through YR-5, were, for the most part, complimentary.
26 The consensus was my audit and accounting skills were quite good and needed no im-
27 provement. Apparently, one partner in each of these evaluations questioned my analytical
28 skills, but I was not given any specific examples of where my analytical skills were lacking.
29 Bill Weisman told me not to worry about that comment because it was from a partner who
30 thought, because I was an online program graduate, I could not be as smart as the other
31 accountants. Bill said although this opinion was unfair, I should just ignore it. He confided in
32 me that he got similar comments before becoming a partner, just because he was the first
33 University of Nita graduate to join C&S. I don't know if Bill was telling me the truth about
34 his receiving bad evaluations, but given his reputation in the firm as one of the best and the
35 brightest, he made me feel better.
36
37 I received another negative comment in one evaluation, I think it was in YR-5, because
38 I couldn't travel on engagements for extended periods of time, due to my child care re-
39 sponsibilities. The commenter felt I was somehow not fulfilling my obligations to the firm.
40 I remember talking with Rachel Levin, a friend from my staff assistant days, and Milton's
41 clerical assistant about the comment and she encouraged me to talk to Milton about it.
42 She said he was fair. I reminded Charles Milton and Ted Potter that I had been hired with
43 the understanding that my travel was limited, that the firm had hired me nonetheless, and
44 that the comment was unfair.

1 I recall one other conversation about this with Milton. I was in Milton's office for some-
2 thing, and he told me the comment about not traveling had been made by a woman part-
3 ner who felt my children were old enough to be left with a childcare provider in the home
4 if I needed to be out of town for an extended period. I think they believed that because a
5 woman made the comment it must be fair. I reminded him I had come to the firm with an
6 understanding my travel would be limited. But this was a very short conversation and really
7 didn't go anywhere. He got a phone call and told me he had to take the call and excused
8 himself, so I left the office. It never came up with Milton again.
9
10 The only women partners at the time I worked at the firm were Danielle Reddick, Sherry
11 Barker, and Ann Feinman who worked in the small business practice, and Cheryl Stein who
12 worked in the tax section. Because I had not worked for anyone other than Ms. Reddick,
13 I assume the comment came from her, even though she never asked me to do any extended
14 travel. As I said, I rarely did any work for her at all.
15
16 The only other negative comment I received in my first four evaluations was "I was not
17 aggressive enough" and I lacked "toughness." When I asked for specific examples, none
18 were forthcoming, but it was a consistent comment. I spoke with Bill Weisman about those
19 comments as well. I remember specifically having a conversation with him after my YR-5
20 evaluation, and he said the "lack of aggressiveness" was a common comment made about
21 women accountants by older male partners and I shouldn't be overly concerned about
22 it. He said the times were changing, but slowly, and the fact that Cheryl Stein had made
23 partner in YR-6 in the tax section, which required taking really aggressive positions with
24 the IRS, was a good sign for my future. He also pointed out women in both the audit and
25 tax sections would be made partner in that year. He said there were just a few of the "old
26 guard" who continued to make such remarks consistently across all the women profes-
27 sionals, but they were aging out and wouldn't be around much longer. Yes, Wanda Kohl
28 and Paula Wells became audit section partners that year. I think one woman became a tax
29 section partner as well, but I don't remember her name. No other women made partner in
30 the audit section for the rest of the time I was there, though.
31
32 My fifth year at the firm as a professional accountant was a particularly difficult one for me.
33 In the fall of YR-5 my father was diagnosed with pancreatic cancer. He only lived for two
34 months after being diagnosed (he died in November of YR-5), and I spent a lot of time trav-
35 eling from Nita City back home to Connecticut. The travel, plus the emotional upheaval,
36 affected my work, both in terms of quantity and quality. Bill Weisman, who had become
37 deputy chair of the audit section (Paul Buckner was now the chair), approached me with
38 some complaints. When I told him what I was going through, he was sympathetic, but told
39 me to use my work as a refuge so I didn't adversely affect my future with the firm.
40
41 That year was also David's junior year in high school and Mina's freshman year. David got
42 involved with a bad group of kids. His grades in the first and second quarter were well be-
43 low normal; he was a solid B+/A student and his grades were in the C range for those quar-
44 ters. Eventually, I caught him with marijuana in his room. We spent a lot of time working

1   through that problem. He responded well, and by the third quarter his grades were into
2   the B/B+ range; by the end of his junior year he was back on track with good grades.
3
4   Mina went through the classic teenage problems all young girls face during that first year
5   of high school. It was especially difficult for us. Her father wasn't there to help her through
6   the time when teenage girls want nothing to do with their mothers. Nonetheless, we
7   weathered the storm and by the summer of YR-4, we were once again a functioning family.
8
9   The effect of all of this was my billable hours were down for that year and the quality of my
10   work also suffered. Even Bill Weisman was less than complimentary about my work. I was
11   trying hard, but with my personal problems, I was just not functioning at anywhere near
12   my normal level.
13
14   My firm evaluation for that year reflected the kind of year I had. The evaluation was held in
15   Paul Buckner's office. Paul had been made the chair of the audit section of the firm in the fall
16   of YR-4. Bill Weisman was also there as the deputy chair. Paul told me that although he and
17   Bill had fought very hard for me, and had asked that my personal problems be considered, my
18   evaluation for my fifth year was a 3. They said there was one other accountant who received a
19   1, two accountants who received 2's, and three other accountants who received 3's. They told
20   me my hours were not acceptable and that, for the first time, they had received some sub-
21   stantial complaints about the quality of my work. They both said they believed I was partner-
22   ship material and I had what it took to make partner, but my 3 evaluation was a real problem.
23
24   Paul told me I had basically three ways to go. First, I could look for a job with another firm
25   and C&S would give excellent recommendations. One of the accountants who received a
26   3 took this option. Second, he could arrange for a very good position for me in the Chief
27   Financial Officer's office of Nita Computer World, which was one of the firm's best corpo-
28   rate clients. He said two other accountants who were evaluated at 3 had chosen to take
29   the option of going to work with a client company, but the Nita Computer World job was
30   the best such position available. Third, I could come to work with him on a major piece of
31   antitrust litigation that was just gearing up on behalf of Nita Computer World, work like
32   hell, and repair my reputation within the firm.
33
34   To me, there was no choice. I chose to work on the Nita Computer World (NCW) litiga-
35   tion with Paul Buckner. I was not a quitter and I had worked too hard to leave C&S under
36   a cloud. I knew many other former accountants with C&S had gone to work for the firm's
37   clients and that the jobs had great security and benefits, but I wasn't willing, at that time
38   in my life, to settle for such a job. Paul said he knew I would choose the third option, but
39   he made it clear my career with C&S was on the line and he expected my best work on the
40   engagement. There were two young partners assigned to the engagement and four other
41   accountants. I was the supervising staff accountant on the NCW engagement.
42
43   The work on the NCW engagement was the most challenging and rewarding account-
44   ing work I had ever done. I use many of the things I learned during that engagement in

1   teaching my complex audit seminar today. I created a simulation roughly based on a sim-
2   plified version of that case to teach recognizing, analyzing, and resolving audit issues. The
3   engagement, which involved an allegation of price fixing on the part of NCW and other dis-
4   tributors of computer hardware and software, was complicated and presented fascinating
5   financial, accounting, and tactical issues that required our input. Paul was right, though.
6   The hours were long and exhausting and, because so much was on the line both for me
7   personally and for the client, I worked harder than I had ever worked before. This was es-
8   pecially so because the judge set a very quick discovery deadline of six months and set the
9   case for a firm trial date in June of YR-3.
10
11   In my position as a supervising staff accountant on the engagement, I helped prepare the
12   lawyers for depositions and drafted the final technical accounting substantive motions and
13   supporting memoranda for Paul's approval and for use by the lawyers (who of course were
14   the final arbiters of what was presented to the court). I was involved in all aspects of case
15   planning and litigation strategy. The NCW engagement only increased my admiration for
16   Paul Buckner as an accountant who also seemed to have a great understanding of the law.
17   His insights were incredible, his instincts sharp, and his ability to analyze data and informa-
18   tion was nothing short of brilliant in my opinion. He was forever in one-on-one consulta-
19   tions with the chief lawyer for NCW in the case.
20
21   As I said, I was involved in all aspects of the engagement relating to accounting and finan-
22   cial matters. I often traveled with Paul or one of the other partners for depositions both in
23   and out of the state. The travel wasn't all that frequent and usually did not involve more
24   than two or three days away from home in a row, so I agreed to the travel. Even though
25   I was a little nervous about leaving the kids, David was being very responsible. He'd re-
26   ceived an early acceptance into the honors program and a partial academic scholarship at
27   Nita University. Mina, after her bad year, seemed to be doing very well both academically
28   and personally. In addition, I knew my career was on the line, so the travel, even though
29   not optimal, was necessary.
30
31   On one of these trips out of town, in January of YR-3, Paul Buckner made his first sexual
32   proposition to me. After a particularly grueling day of prepping lawyers to take depositions
33   and then a long preparation session in his room on the items on the next day's agenda,
34   Paul ordered up a late-night meal with some wine and we sat and relaxed. Talk turned to
35   our personal lives. Paul asked about the kids and I told him they were doing well. He asked
36   how I was doing. I told him how happy I was working on the NCW engagement, and he said
37   my work was first-rate and my prospects for partnership were looking better every day. He
38   then asked about my social life, and although it was none of his business, I told him that
39   between the job and the kids, I had no social life. Paul started talking about his marriage
40   and his kids. He said he and his wife were married only in name, and they only stayed mar-
41   ried for his children, the youngest of whom was a high school senior.
42
43   Although I was uncomfortable with the conversation, I was exhausted from work, and the
44   closeness of our working relationship made the conversation feel—if not natural, sort of

1   inevitable—people who work together talk about their lives, you know? Paul made some

2   comment about how different I was from his wife. He said she seemed to care about noth-

3   ing other than her social standing and really cared little for him or their children. He said

4   he admired me for what I had accomplished, both professionally and with my children. At

5   some point during the conversation he got up and walked around the back of my chair and

6   started to massage my shoulders. Although this made me more than a little uncomfort-

7   able, it felt good, so I didn't protest. Then he kissed me on the neck. Although I shouldn't

8   have been, given Paul's reputation, I was surprised, and I jumped up out of my chair.

9

10 Paul seemed shocked by my reaction, but I just said I wasn't ready for that kind of relation-

11 ship, and I should probably leave. He told me there was no need for that; he was attracted

12 to me, but he had misread my signals. He apologized for being so forward. I sat back in

13 the chair and we talked about the case and the next day's deposition prep for about a half

14 hour. I then went back to my room.

15

16 The next day Paul was very cool and formal with me. I guess I bruised his fragile male ego.

17 I assumed things would get back to normal between us as the case continued at its break-

18 neck pace and, after a couple of more days of the silent treatment, our working relation-

19 ship was back to normal. In March, we were out of town on another set of depositions,

20 and again were meeting in his room after a long day. After we finished our business, Paul

21 asked if I was interested in a little relaxation and conversation. When I hesitated, he said

22 something like "just conversation," and I relaxed and agreed to share a late supper and a

23 glass of wine with him.

24

25 Paul was particularly talkative, and after inquiring after my family and me, he talked about

26 his relationship with his family. He again complained about his wife having more concern

27 for her country club and social gatherings than him and his children. He told me his mar-

28 riage, which had lasted over twenty-five years, had been nothing more than a shell for the

29 last fifteen. He asked me if I was aware of the rumors about him and other women and I

30 admitted I was. He didn't deny them, but explained them away as his searching for some-

31 thing better. He told me once his son (his youngest) graduated from high school that June,

32 he was going to file for divorce. He said he had thought about divorce before but, when he

33 talked to his wife, she made it very clear that he would have a hard time seeing the children

34 and she would use his affairs to ensure his access to the children was severely limited. Ac-

35 cording to Paul, his relationship with his children was strained at best, because of his long

36 hours at work and long periods of time away from home, and he didn't want to lose what

37 little relationship he had with them. He hoped as they matured, he could have an adult

38 relationship with them, something he very much wanted.

39

40 He also said that when he was younger, he worried about the effect a divorce would have

41 on his career, given many of his corporate clients were controlled by social friends who

42 were originally friends of his wife and her family. He said he now understood that although

43 social relationships may open doors, corporate decisions are made on sound business

44 bases, not on social friendship. He said he was now confident his clients would remain with

1   him regardless of whether he and his wife divorced, so he was ready to go forward with the
2   divorce. In fact, he said, the only thing keeping him going was his work; his only regret was
3   he didn't have someone special to share it with.
4
5   To be honest, I was moved by what Paul had to say. He seemed so sad about his life, which
6   from my perspective seemed so glamorous. I really wanted to hug him, but what had hap-
7   pened before between us stopped me, I guess. I told him I was sure everything would work
8   out for him, that I hoped it would. He smiled at me in sort of a sad way and said he hoped
9   so, too. And that was that. He changed the topic back to the NCW case.
10
11   That night was the beginning of a different relationship between Paul Buckner and me.
12   Although he didn't attempt anything physical, at the end of long days both on the road and
13   in Nita City, we would often have long talks about the most personal of things. We were not
14   intimate sexually, but we were intimate. He told me all about himself and his life and I did
15   likewise. We spent an enormous amount of time together through the conclusion of the NCW
16   engagement in early June of YR-3; the case settled on very favorable terms for our client, NCW.
17   The engagement was also a personal success. I was uniformly praised for my work on the en-
18   gagement, in particular for my work with one of the lawyers, a senior trial lawyer (number
19   2 on the case) on a protective order concerning some trade secrets of NCW's that was eventu-
20   ally granted by the court. I received a copy of a letter the Vice President and General Counsel
21   of NCW wrote to Paul that acknowledged my contributions to the case. (See Exhibit 6.)
22
23   NCW was so pleased with the outcome, worth over 10 million dollars to NCW and appar-
24   ently much better than expected, that they gave the members of the litigation team a trip,
25   with spouses, for a week in the Bahamas. Everyone on the team, including all the accoun-
26   tants, were invited. Because I wasn't married and because Paul apparently never went
27   anywhere with his wife, we were the only people there without a significant other. On
28   our third night there, one thing led to another and Paul and I ended up sleeping together.
29   I should have known it was the wrong thing to do, but it happened anyway. We spent a
30   terrific week together and Paul started talking about our future together.
31
32   I know sometime during the week I asked Paul about when his son was going to graduate
33   from high school. He told me the boy needed to attend summer school in order to finish his
34   degree and that he had pulled some strings to get him into college. Paul then volunteered
35   that as soon as his boy was firmly in school he was going to file for divorce. I know I should
36   have recognized he was repeating the pattern I heard he had with other women, but I
37   wanted our relationship to work. It was, after all, the only serious relationship I had with
38   a man other than my husband. I rationalized that this time Paul was different. First, unlike
39   his other conquests I was not young. I was in my late thirties and the other women had all
40   been in their twenties. Second, the way our relationship came about seemed so natural
41   that I was sure he was sincere. Third, the rumors about Paul had lessened in recent years
42   and I guess I wanted to believe he had changed. Finally, the last kid being out of the house
43   seemed like a good time to end a bad relationship and, from everything he said, he truly
44   had a bad relationship with his wife.

1   The rest of that summer flew by. I was extremely happy with both my job and my personal
2   life. My kids were doing great. They met Paul and liked him. I didn't think they knew about
3   my relationship with him, but as I later learned, they knew exactly what was going on.
4   I told Paul that in light of my personal relationship with him, I thought I shouldn't work with
5   him unless he absolutely needed me; he agreed. That summer I got terrific assignments,
6   better than ever before. The engagements were exciting, and I was asked to work on in-
7   teresting issues. My relationship with Paul was also terrific. We spent time away from the
8   office together, including some weekend getaways. The only problem I had was Labor Day
9   weekend when he said he had to spend it with his wife's family at some gathering in Mar-
10 tha's Vineyard. Paul told me he really didn't want to go, but it was the last chance he had to
11 be with his son before he went off to school; his other kids would also be there, including
12 his oldest daughter who had just had her first child, a son. So even though I wasn't happy
13 about it, I didn't put up a fuss about his going. I spent the weekend with my kids instead,
14 and we had a wonderful time.
15
16 I had my sixth-year evaluation right after Labor Day in YR-3. It was again held in Paul's of-
17 fice, with Bill Weisman also there. I was thrilled when Paul told me my evaluation for the
18 year was a 1. He said the partners in the audit section were very impressed with all the ter-
19 rific work I did on the NCW engagement and with the enormous number of hours I billed
20 for the year. He also said the management people at NCW were pleased with my work and
21 they would be pleased to have me work on other engagements for them, as would their
22 lawyers, apparently both on NCW litigation and for other clients, which was consistent
23 with the letter NCW sent to Paul. (See Exhibit 6.) Finally they told me that of my group of
24 staff accountants, only one other person was evaluated at the 1 level, and it looked very
25 good for me for a positive partnership vote in the spring of YR-2. I was on cloud nine. Paul
26 came out of his chair and gave me a big hug and a kiss. Because Bill was in the room, I was
27 a little embarrassed, but at the time nothing could have upset me. I do remember telling
28 Paul that in the future we should not have any public displays of affection in the office;
29 I thought it was unprofessional, and others might hold it against me. Paul agreed with me,
30 but said at some point the people in the firm would have to get used to it.
31
32 In fact, the day after my evaluation Bill Weisman came to my office and asked if I minded a
33 little advice from an old friend. I, of course, was interested in what he had to say. Bill asked
34 if I was aware of Paul's sexual history with women in the firm. I told him I was, but Paul had
35 told me once his son was away at college, he was leaving his wife. When Bill started to say
36 something like, "he's said that before," I told him I didn't want to talk about my relationship
37 with Paul. Bill backed off, but did say he hoped things worked out for me but, if they didn't,
38 he wasn't sure he could protect me at the firm. His statement sort of shook me, but I didn't
39 respond. I felt I had weathered the storm at the firm by way of long hours and hard work, and
40 that was all the protection I needed. I'll have to admit what Bill said was unsettling and made
41 me feel somewhat vulnerable, but I certainly didn't realize how vulnerable I turned out to be.
42
43 In September of YR-3, I started work on another engagement for NCW. It wasn't of the same
44 size in dollar terms or complexity, but it was nonetheless interesting. Bill Weisman was the

1   partner in charge of the engagement, although Paul retained supervisory control over all the
2   firm's work for NCW. As a result, when I had to travel to some of NCW's offices out of state,
3   Paul, who was not involved in any special case at the time, sometimes came along. On one
4   of these trips in late September or early October, I had a conversation with Paul about his
5   marital status. When I asked whether he had seen a lawyer about his divorce, he got angry
6   and snapped out something like, "the marriage lasted over twenty-five years, it takes some
7   time to end it," but then he calmed down almost immediately and said it was important for
8   his son to be into his school routine before hitting him with that kind of news. He said the boy
9   needed a semester to get adjusted. I appreciated that his son had some academic problems
10   in high school, and that college took some adjustment, so I accepted Paul's explanation.
11
12   I got heavily involved in the NCW engagement and was working hard on it with Bill. Bill
13   never asked directly about my relationship with Paul, but he occasionally asked how things
14   were going for me. Even though by late fall I was questioning whether Paul would ever
15   leave his wife, I never said anything about it to Bill.
16
17   The Christmas holidays spelled the end of my relationship with Paul Buckner. We got into
18   a fight in early December about where Paul was spending Christmas Day. He wanted to
19   spend Christmas and the week after Christmas on vacation with his family—including his
20   wife, his children, and their families—at his home in Palm Beach, Florida. He told me it
21   was one of the only times he got to see kids and even though he preferred to be with me,
22   he thought he should spend one last holiday with his family before his divorce. I was very
23   unhappy about his plans, but Paul promised me that at the end of the vacation, he would
24   spend an extra day in Florida with his wife and tell her he was getting a divorce. This made
25   me feel better, but of course he never did ask for the divorce.
26
27   Paul returned to Nita City right after the first of the year and came over to my house to see
28   me. Fortunately my kids were out, because when I asked him how his wife took the divorce
29   news, Paul told me he hadn't said anything to her about the divorce. I got very angry and
30   started shouting at him. He asked me to calm down, which took some time. He told me
31   he was still going to ask for the divorce, but his son was having a rough time adjusting to
32   school and he wanted to wait until the boy had finished his freshman year before subject-
33   ing him to the upheaval of a divorce. I wanted to believe Paul, but I was still very angry.
34   I made him leave.
35
36   Over the next week, Paul was out of town on business. He called several times and sent
37   flowers, but I didn't return his calls. I spent most of the week trying to figure out what
38   I was going to do and concluded that even though I wanted him to, Paul was probably
39   never going to leave his wife. I decided to give him one last chance. When he returned to
40   Nita City, I invited him to my house for dinner. This would have been around January 15.
41   I told him how I felt and that if he loved me and wanted to be with me he had to get a law-
42   yer and get divorce proceedings started in one week. He started to protest about his son,
43   and I told him I didn't want to hear about his son; it was time for Paul to decide what he
44   really wanted. I then sent him home and told him to call me with his decision.

1   The next week crawled by. The stress must have shown on me because several people
2   asked me if I was well. That weekend Paul came to my house. He asked if I wanted to go
3   away with him for a vacation in the Bahamas and pulled out some plane tickets from his
4   pocket. I assumed he had told his wife he wanted a divorce. I ran to hug him and asked how
5   she took the news. Paul told me to take it easy, but it hadn't happened yet. I pushed him
6   away and asked him to leave. He tried to hold onto the hug, but I twisted away and ordered
7   him to get the hell out of my house. That's when he got really angry. I'll never forget the
8   fury on his face as he turned to walk out the door. As he left, he said, "You're all the same.
9   You don't realize when you've got a good thing going. You'll regret this, I promise you."
10   Those words and anger are forever in my memory.

11

12   That's the last conversation I had with Paul Buckner for about two months. He went off to
13   work as an expert witness on an engagement in Seattle. He never emailed or called. Ap-
14   parently, our breakup didn't affect him much because his testimony went well, and they
15   won the case. When he returned to Nita City, he called to ask me to dinner, but I refused.
16   I had spent the time he was away trying to get over Paul; I didn't want to chance getting
17   involved with him again. The next two months was very hard for me. I had trouble con-
18   centrating on assignments in the beginning, but eventually I came around and immersed
19   myself in my work. My health was another matter. Between the stress, the lack of sleep,
20   and the fact that I wasn't eating particularly well, I caught a series of colds and viruses,
21   some of which were bad enough to keep me out of work. They continued well into the
22   spring of YR-2.

23

24   Because of my health, I welcomed the fact that my assignments lightened up in the winter
25   and early spring of YR-2, and I wasn't very busy. That was only a portent of things to come.

26

27   In May of YR-2, Bill Weisman asked me to come to his office. When I got there, Bill said
28   the firm's partners would be considering three staff accountants for partnership, and if
29   I wanted, I too could be included for consideration. I asked for his advice, and he said he
30   thought it might be a good idea to put off the partnership decision for a year or so. That
31   surprised me, and I asked him why. He said various partners would bring up the drop-off
32   in my production and the lingering problems some people had with my online MBA pro-
33   gram background, my early refusal to travel, and my lack of toughness, so partners who
34   didn't know me well could be hesitant to vote for me. Putting off the partnership decision
35   for another year could improve my chances. I asked Bill whether this was Paul's doing. He
36   deflected my question by telling me this was his best advice, but he was willing to fight for
37   me if I desired. He said to think it over for a couple of days and get back to him.

38

39   Over the weekend I went through all the options in my head. Paul was obviously doing to
40   me what he'd done to his other former lovers. I realized the drop off in my assignments
41   was no accident and, while I felt fortunate for a break in my assignments, the lack of as-
42   signments was designed to hurt me. No, I didn't protest the lack of work to anyone. I just
43   viewed it as a cyclical thing. I had been very busy in the fall, working on the second NCW
44   engagement with Bill and several other matters.

1   My billables for September, YR-3 through January, YR-2 were approximately 850 hours,
2   which on average was better than my previous year. After speaking with Bill, I checked my
3   billables for February, YR-2 through May, YR-2 and they were only 550 hours. I'll admit that
4   wasn't very good, but it wasn't insurmountable. Even bearing in mind the time I needed to
5   rebuild my work load, I know I could have billed 700 hours in the last four months to end up
6   with a respectable 2,100 hours for the year, assuming I got decent assignments. The firm's
7   benchmark for accountants is 2,200 billable hours a year with 80 percent collectables. That
8   might have been a stretch, but I could have gotten close.
9
10 After considering this math, I concluded I was better off coming up for partnership in that
11 year—while my NCW success was still fresh in everyone's mind—than waiting for a year of
12 reduced assignments and letting them drive me out that way. I gave Bill my decision and,
13 although he tried to talk me out of it, he promised to go forward.
14
15 About a week later, Bill came to my office and gave me the bad news: I didn't make it out
16 of the audit section with a recommendation of partnership. He said it was close, but I had
17 just missed. He told me the firm was giving me six months to find another position. I was
18 obviously very upset. I asked Bill if Paul spoke in favor of me. Bill said the meeting was
19 confidential and he couldn't tell me who said what. He did say he was sure Paul would
20 give me a good reference if I wanted one. He said he was sorry. I also asked Bill how the
21 three others who were up for partnership had fared. He told me Roger Kramer and Mark
22 Hancock had made partner, and Michael DeAngelo had decided to put off consideration
23 for partnership for a year. I asked if I could come up again in the next year, and Bill told me
24 once an accountant chose to go forward, as I did, there was no turning back. He doubted a
25 new vote would make any difference.
26
27 My treatment by C&S left me hurt and angry, and convinced dumping Paul Buckner
28 caused them to deny my partnership. I decided I should do something about it. After
29 some research, I learned that complaining to the Equal Employment Opportunity Com-
30 mission (EEOC) was a necessary prerequisite to bringing suit against C&S. I went to the
31 Nita EEOC office to file a complaint. The interviewer expressed sympathy, but said she
32 was unlikely to get to my claim for a long while. She told me to contact her in 180 days
33 so she could issue a "Right to Sue" letter if I wanted to pursue my claim in the courts.
34 I did so, and received a form giving me the right to sue in December of YR-2, shortly after
35 I resigned from C&S.
36
37 I took some time off to sort through my career options. During this period, I considered
38 changing career paths, but nothing really caught my fancy. I sent out some resumes, but
39 nothing came of it. Several firms seemed to be interested initially and had me send refer-
40 ence letters, but only a couple of firms gave me what I would consider a full interview, and
41 no job offer was made. Because I didn't have a portfolio of business to bring to a new firm,
42 my prospects to be a partner in a large firm in Nita City didn't seem great. What did sur-
43 prise me was that I didn't receive any senior accountant offers. I thought about moving to
44 another city, but Nita had been my home and I really didn't want to leave.

1 One evening I received an alumni newsletter in the mail from Nita University, and I started
2 to think about teaching as a career. The next day I called Gary Sherman, who had been a
3 senior accountant at C&S and who had left for a teaching career several years before. He
4 was very helpful, but frankly discouraging about a position as a tenure track faculty mem-
5 ber at the Nita University Business School or at Conwell. Although both schools offered
6 online MBA programs, the degree was not valued in business schools, mainly populated by
7 Ivy League MBAs. He advised me that law schools were hiring people on their faculties
8 whose ultimate academic degree was not in law. This was especially so for candidates with
9 related PhD degrees, especially in economics. Law schools also offered positions for "prac-
10 tice professors," who taught courses of two sorts: courses related to litigation for lawyers
11 with substantial practice experience but little interest in the academics of law school, espe-
12 cially with regard to scholarship; and courses in related professional areas such as law and
13 medicine (sometimes taught by nurse practitioners) and the intersection of law and ac-
14 counting. He recommended I work some interesting project from practice into prospective
15 teaching materials before the university law school hiring process started in the fall of YR-2.
16
17 Although I valued Gary's advice, I looked into positions at business schools. There was,
18 indeed, an apparent bias in hiring online graduates onto business school faculties, even
19 though I had graduated first in my class and summa cum laude. I got the same feedback as
20 I received from Gary from several of my professors at the Nita University Business School,
21 who were pessimistic about a business school appointment but endorsed the practice pro-
22 fessor idea for law schools. They uniformly thought I was well qualified for such a position
23 and encouraged me to apply to the Nita Law School, which they understood was open to
24 such positions. I also sent out resumes to approximately twenty-five business schools and
25 got absolutely no interest in my joining a business school faculty.
26
27 Gary introduced me to a professor at the law school, Mary Fahad. She met with me,
28 looked at my resume, and suggested some changes to highlight experience that would
29 appeal to a law school (emphasizing my forensic work). She agreed I should look initially
30 at a practice professor position and, if I developed a scholarly interest and produced at
31 a high level while teaching at a high level, transfer to a tenure eligible position down
32 the line. She asked about my experience a C&S. I told her my tale of woe and that I was
33 thinking of suing for gender discrimination. She, being a Muslim and an Arab, asked if
34 I thought race or religion had any impact on their decision. Although I didn't think so, C&S
35 employed no other professional CPAs with Middle Eastern names. I didn't know if any of
36 the black employees were also Muslim. As it turned out, there was some anti-Muslim
37 feeling in the firm, but it was from individuals. One person, as I found out when looking
38 at the exhibits, had to be chastised for inappropriate remarks. When I asked Bill, he said
39 they had received a comment during the evaluation process from one partner who said
40 he didn't want any terrorists in burkas in the firm. Now those words do not appear, but
41 I understand that was the reference to an inappropriate conduct in Exhibit 3D-1. Mary
42 assured me there was no such problem at the law school and I needn't worry about my
43 lawsuit's impact on my job status, which turned out to be true with several faculty mem-
44 bers offering advice on my lawsuit.

1   The more I thought of it, the more the practice professor position at a law school ap-
2   pealed to me. At C&S, I got the most enjoyment out of my forensic work and thought
3   I would enjoy teaching to students the things I taught the lawyers with whom I had
4   worked. I thought I could marry that experience with the problem method used by many
5   of my business school instructors and create some interesting and thoughtful teaching
6   problems for a course. And while I know you have to wait until you are a senior partner
7   in a practice, it was frustrating never getting to see the big picture, never finishing the
8   investigation into some of the interesting intellectual issues that arise at the conflu-
9   ence of accounting and law—no one is going to pay an accountant to go beyond what
10   was necessary to deal with a client's problems. Those issues could provide fodder for
11   academic writing that might get me onto the tenure track. In addition, although my
12   kids were still in school, and you can make a lot more money in private practice, my life
13   style didn't demand a huge salary. So even though I would take a substantial pay cut,
14   I thought I should explore the teaching option. It was late in my career for such a move,
15   but I thought exploring the practice professor option was worth the effort. Working at
16   the University of Nita Law School was my first choice, because both my kids were inter-
17   ested in careers living and working in the Nita City area and I wanted to stay close to
18   them, physically and otherwise.
19
20   The next week at the office, I started working on a forensic accounting survey course and
21   the "problem/simulation" method for teaching the course. I also identified potential top-
22   ics for future scholarly articles. My work assignments had dwindled, so there was little to
23   distract me. By early fall I had outlined a basic survey course in forensic auditing and pre-
24   pared the problem/simulation method materials for that course. Working on the course
25   outline was one of the most satisfying intellectual experiences of my career and confirmed
26   I should continue to pursue a position at the Nita Law School as suggested by Professor
27   Fahad.
28
29   My interest in a practice professor position matched up with a need at Nita Law School
30   and after teaching Accounting for Lawyers as an adjunct for the winter YR-1 semester,
31   I was offered and accepted a practice professor position beginning in fall semester YR-1.
32   My starting salary at the law school was $75,000, and in the first academic year I taught
33   two sections of Accounting for Lawyers (a basic survey course on all aspects of account-
34   ing relevant to law practice), and Forensic Accounting Basics. My agreement was to add a
35   seminar in Advanced Forensic Accounting to my teaching load.
36
37   The law school offer came at a good time for me; I needed an ego boost to restore some
38   of the self-esteem I lost in my unsuccessful search for accounting jobs in Nita City. As
39   I said, I had applied to several accounting firms, beginning in the summer of YR-2, but no
40   positions came open for me. I had a number of interviews but received no offers. Initially,
41   I thought the whole experience at C&S had demoralized me, and I was not coming across
42   as very confident in interviews, or my foray into academic writing had steered me towards
43   an academic career, which had diminished my enthusiasm in accounting firm job inter-
44   views. Instead, my real problem with accounting firm jobs was Paul Buckner.

1 Bill Weisman told me in June of YR-2 that he had written me a glowing recommendation
2 for Paul Buckner's signature, and I should feel free to use both him and Paul as references
3 when looking for an accounting position. Although I hesitated to use Paul as a reference, I
4 did so after Bill showed me a copy of the letter he drafted for Paul's signature. (See Exhibit
5 10.) Just after the first of the year in YR-1 I got a phone call from a friend of mine at Mor-
6 rison & Farrow, an accounting firm in Nita City to which I had applied in June or July of YR-2.
7 This friend told me she had seen Paul Buckner's recommendation letter and it was unflat-
8 tering, to say the least. She also told me Morrison & Farrow's hiring partner, John Randall,
9 spoke with Paul about me, and Paul was very negative in his evaluation of my abilities. She
10 gave me a copy of Paul's letter from their files; it is obviously not a good letter of recom-
11 mendation and not consistent with my performance at C&S. (See Exhibit 11.) I recognize
12 the handwriting at the bottom of the page on Exhibit 11, that says to "be careful," as Paul
13 Buckner's. He deep-sixed me with Morrison & Farrow. I can only assume he did the same
14 with other firms who inquired of him, which explains why I received no accounting firm
15 job offers.
16
17 I stayed on at C&S until the end of my six-month grace period, just to save some more
18 money. I turned in my resignation to Bill Weisman. Bill was very supportive of me in my job
19 search, both in practice and academia. Although he tried to get excited about the practice
20 professor position at the law school, I could tell he was disappointed for me. He inquired
21 about my finances and offered to loan me money if I needed it. I told him I appreciated
22 his concern, but I would be all right. I had cashed in my retirement account at C&S, which
23 more than covered me for the short term when combined with my salary as an adjunct at
24 the law school.
25
26 After the EEOC notified C&S about my complaint against them, Bill offered to give what-
27 ever testimony he could about my time at C&S. Since my resignation from the firm, I have
28 had dinner with Bill on a few occasions. He has been a good friend to me. We don't often
29 talk about C&S, but Bill did tell me in late YR-2 or early YR-1 that he had become disen-
30 chanted with the firm and firm politics.
31
32 In January of YR-1, I told Bill what Paul had done to me when I had applied for accounting
33 firm jobs. He was visibly upset. He confronted Paul, who admitted he had indeed written
34 his own reference letter, which was far from complimentary, and sent it to all the firms
35 that requested my references. When Bill called me with that news, he also told me he
36 was considering leaving the firm for a position with NCW. In the end, Bill was appointed
37 Vice President and CFO of Nita Computer World. He started with them in April of YR-1.
38 Shortly after beginning at NCW, Bill and I had one of our dinners. He offered me a position
39 in NCW's CFO's office to assist in managing the financial matters of the company, and to
40 be NCW's representative in commercial litigation, ensuring outside litigators' command of
41 accounting issues was up to snuff. Although I was flattered by the offer, I had accepted the
42 fulltime position at the law school. Even though the NCW job would have paid a starting
43 salary of $90,000, and my law school salary started at $75,000, I wanted to give teaching a
44 good try. In fact, during my semester as an adjunct I published a law review article entitled

1 *Ultimate Issue Accounting Opinions in Antitrust Litigation* (64 Conwell Law Review 38,
2 YR-1), which received positive reviews from my colleagues at the law school. Professor
3 Fahad (who became dean of the law school in January, YR-0) opined that if I could show a
4 regular commitment to quality scholarship (an article every nine to eighteen months), in
5 a couple of years a transfer to the tenure track faculty was not out of the question. That
6 would mean a significant raise to as much as $135,000.
7
8 Although I am very happy at the law school, I do miss the different challenges and the highs
9 and lows of audit accounting. I worked very hard to succeed at C&S and deserved to be
10 treated better than I was. I believe my failure to receive a partnership offer was a direct re-
11 sult of my breaking off my relationship with Paul Buckner and perhaps some discrimination
12 based on my religion and ethnicity. I also believe C&S discriminates against women. Only
13 one (in YR-1) woman has ever been made a partner in the audit section, which is the most
14 prestigious area of the firm's practice. The only women partners were either Danielle's
15 small business group, where in addition to Danielle there are two other women partners
16 (Sherry Barker and Ann Feinman) and in the tax section which has only two women part-
17 ners (Cheryl Stein and Kathryn Kowalski).
18
19 I also believe Paul Buckner slandered me when talking to people at firms where I applied
20 for accountant positions after being forced out of C&S. Although his letter (see Exhibit 11)
21 is not negative in an absolute sense, it is not a fair representation of my work at the firm,
22 and certainly is not the kind of letter on which you base a positive hiring decision. In ad-
23 dition, his oral statements, at least to John Randall at Morrison & Farrow (see Exhibit 18),
24 were out-and-out false.

I have read this deposition and it is complete and accurate.

Kiya Ahmed
Kiya Ahmed

Subscribed and sworn before me this 10th day of July, YR-0.

Harry Gibbons
Harry Gibbons
Certified Shorthand Reporter

This deposition was taken in the office of the counsel for the defendants on June 24th,
YR-0. This deposition was given under oath and was read and signed by the deponent.

DEPOSITION OF BILL WEISMAN

1 My name is Bill Weisman. I am forty-three years old and work as the Vice President and
2 Chief Financial Officer of Nita Computer World, which is a national wholesaler and re-
3 tailer of computers and other electronic equipment. Until April 1st of YR-I, I was a partner
4 at the firm of Cooper & Stewart (C&S) in Nita City. For the period YR-4 until the time I left
5 the firm, I was the deputy chair of the audit section of the firm. I divorced my wife, Gerry,
6 in YR-14. Fortunately, we did not have any children.
7
8 I was born and raised in Nita City and graduated from the public schools. I have six sib-
9 lings, all but two of whom still live in the area. My brother Mike lives in Los Angeles and
10 my sister Carol lives in Atlanta. My parents still live in Nita City. My father is a retired
11 postal worker. My mother still teaches part-time at Nita Community College.
12
13 I received my undergraduate degree in accounting from Bucknell University in Lewisburg,
14 Pennsylvania, in YR-20 where I was an academic scholarship student. I graduated with
15 honors. I have always wanted to be an accountant, and to do that I needed an extra year
16 of university level training and some additional course work. Accounting requires five
17 years of university level training, not just four. So, I decided to do an MBA and get the ex-
18 tra degree along with the extra two years of academic work. Although I was accepted by
19 several so-called top business schools, none of them offered me any substantial financial
20 aid, so when I was accepted to the University of Nita Business School, I decided to take
21 advantage of the in-state tuition and enrolled in September of YR-20. I married Gerry in
22 the summer of YR-20. She also graduated from Bucknell, which is where we met.
23
24 While I was doing my MBA program, Gerry attended Nita University, pursuing a PhD in
25 philosophy. She got her PhD in YR-18. Gerry's job opportunities were somewhat limited
26 in the Nita area, but I wanted to stay in Nita City. Gerry turned down some very attractive
27 offers elsewhere and took a job in Nita City. I always felt guilty about that decision, and
28 Gerry resented me. This was especially so when I received an offer from C&S, one of the
29 best firms in the region. Gerry felt she had sacrificed in her career for me, while I never
30 had to sacrifice anything in my career for her—and she was right. As an accountant,
31 I could have gone anywhere, while her options were limited. I still regret, at times, that
32 I didn't take her needs into consideration; I put my career before my wife, and as a re-
33 sult I lost her. We separated in YR-15 and eventually divorced in YR-14. Gerry now lives
34 and works in Brooklyn, where she is a chaired, tenured full professor in the Philosophy
35 Department at Fordham University.
36
37 To be honest, I was surprised I ended up at C&S. Although I had a good record in my grad-
38 uate program, graduating first in my class, C&S had the reputation of being an elitist ac-
39 counting firm. I was the first Nita University MBA graduate ever to receive an offer from
40 them. Even though I had offers from some of the other large accounting firms in the city
41 for the summer during my business school tenure, I chose to go to C&S to prove to them
42 that Nita University really is a fine school. Perhaps because of that, I worked especially

1   hard. I must have made a good impression because C&S offered me a position as a staff
2   accountant with the firm in YR-17, which I accepted. Aside from the honor of being the
3   first Nita grad, the other reason I accepted C&S's offer was Paul Buckner.
4

5   During my summer job at C&S the year before I finished my MBA program, I was assigned
6   to work with Paul Buckner on a routine audit involving two related Nita City companies. He
7   gave me interesting work to do, and always took the time to explain how what I was doing
8   fit into the whole of the engagement. He also invited me along on client meetings. I found
9   the experience fascinating, so when Paul praised my work and urged me to come on board
10   at C&S, my decision was made. I took and passed the CPA exam on the first try. I completed
11   the required one-year internship at another Nita City firm, Brinks and Staten, and became
12   a licensed CPA. C&S hired me back as a staff accountant as soon as I had my license.
13

14   Paul Buckner became my mentor at the firm. He helped me get the right assignments
15   and avoid the political pitfalls that exist in every accounting firm. He also took a special
16   interest in my work and development. Whenever Paul was involved in a high-profile en-
17   gagement, he requested I be assigned to work with him. I had no family responsibilities,
18   so was always available for business travel. While I was a staff accountant, Paul became
19   recognized as one of the leading rainmakers, attracting lots of business in the firm. With
20   Paul's guidance, I was fast-tracked through the staff accountant process and became a
21   partner in the firm in YR-11, a year before anyone else in the group of accountants who
22   began with me, and a year before the earliest partnership decisions at C&S are normally
23   made. Paul was not only responsible for training me and assigning me good work to do,
24   he was the driving force in my being made a partner, at least on the fast-track basis.
25

26   While Paul Buckner is a role model for me as an accountant, he does have his Achilles'
27   heel. Although he is married with four children, Paul is well known in the firm for having
28   extramarital affairs with young women in the office. This was especially so in my early
29   years at the firm. It seemed every few months another rumor would circulate about an
30   affair with a clerical assistant, staff assistant, or accountant. I don't have much specific
31   information, but I do know of several instances when I was either approached by the
32   young woman involved or where the affair was public.
33

34   One such public affair was with a staff assistant by the name of Ellen Dorsen. She and
35   Paul had a relationship that lasted some six months or so, during YR-12 and maybe car-
36   rying over into YR-11. Ms. Dorsen was quite public about the relationship and spoke
37   openly about how she and Paul were doing this or that together. I also overheard her say
38   Paul was going to leave his wife to marry her. According to the rumor mill, that was Paul's
39   modus operandi: promise to get a divorce, and then fail to go through with the promise,
40   which led to the end of the relationship. Paul and Ms. Dorsen eventually broke up; she
41   was working on an engagement with me at the time, and I had to ask she be removed
42   from the engagement. Her work suddenly became very sloppy, which was not the norm
43   for her, and never came back to her standards. The firm eventually let her go.
44

1   I am also personally aware of two affairs Paul had with young women accountants.
2   I know he was involved for a brief time in YR-11 with Karen Newman, who was a fourth-
3   year accountant with the firm. Karen was well regarded in the firm, but generally not
4   considered partnership material. In the normal course of things, I expect she would have
5   left the firm within a year of when she did, but I suspect her affair with Paul Buckner
6   hastened her leaving. She and Paul worked briefly together on an engagement that took
7   them to Dallas with some frequency. Because I was not involved in that engagement,
8   I only became aware of their sexual relationship after the fact when Karen approached
9   me to get some advice.
10
11 She told me she had a brief affair with Paul Buckner but broke it off when it became ob-
12 vious to her that he had no intention of leaving his wife. She complained to me that her
13 work assignments had dropped off both in terms of quantity (she was having a hard time
14 keeping her billable hours up) and quality (she was assigned to work on several small
15 business matters, which were not considered prestige work within the firm). She was
16 afraid Paul Buckner was sabotaging her. She came to me because of my relationship with
17 Paul, which was public knowledge. I did not believe Paul would do such a thing, and I told
18 her so. I did counsel her about her career; she felt she had no realistic opportunity to
19 make partner at C&S and I suggested that a fourth-year accountant had very marketable
20 skills and she should consider moving earlier rather than later. I promised to write a letter
21 on her behalf and ask Paul to do so as well. When I asked Paul to write a recommendation
22 for Karen, he told me to draft something for his signature and he was glad to help. Shortly
23 thereafter Karen left the firm for a position with another firm in Nita City.
24
25 The only other relationship between Paul and a staff accountant about which I have first-
26 hand knowledge, other than with Kiya Ahmed, was with Carol Merritt. Carol was assigned
27 to one of Paul's engagements in YR-10, on which I was also working. The engagement in-
28 volved some paper mills in Washington State and a claim by an environmentalist group
29 that the company falsified its accounting records on the harvesting of substantial forests
30 to avoid EPA sanctions. We spent quite a bit of time in YR-10 in Washington working on
31 this matter. Carol was a fourth-year accountant and was one of two accountants assigned
32 to drill down into the backup data and records and essentially manage the engagement.
33 Although she was married, and the engagement took her away from home for at least
34 four days of every week, she seemed to enjoy the work and did a great job.
35   ~Cauhas
36 Early in the engagement, Paul and Carol began a relationship. They were circumspect in
37 the beginning, but as time went on became quite public about their affair, at least while
38 they were in Washington. I never saw them together in Nita City, although I heard that
39 she had taken an apartment separate from her husband, which she shared intermittently
40 with Paul. The affair between Carol and Paul lasted through the work in Washington
41 and, when that engagement ended in late YR-10 or early YR-9, the relationship ended
42 shortly thereafter. Carol took it quite hard; she took about a month's leave from the
43 firm. I know Paul felt bad about the situation because he called me into his office and
44 explained that Carol had decided not to rejoin the firm. He said he regretted what had

1   happened between them, but it was just one of those things. He said Carol was back with
2   her husband and they were moving to Washington, DC. He asked me to write some glow-
3   ing recommendations for her, based on her work in the Washington engagement (which
4   was quite good) and send them to a list of his friends in various DC firms. I also wrote to
5   some friends of mine and within a few months Carol had joined a very good firm in DC.
6   I believe she's a partner there now and doing quite well.
7
8   Other than his affair with Kiya Ahmed, I have no other specific information about Paul
9   Buckner's alleged extramarital activity with people in the firm. There was a rumor about
10 a relationship with someone at one of the banks in the city in YR-8, but that was just a
11 rumor. In fact, in the years before his relationship with Kiya, the rumors about Paul's af-
12 fairs tapered off, as far as I know. But given my relationship with Paul, I don't think people
13 would consider me a good person with whom to share such gossip. On the other hand,
14 we still work together from time to time; if Paul had a serious affair, especially with some-
15 one in the firm, I think I would have heard about it. In YR-7 Paul's son was in a bad car
16 accident that seriously threatened his life. Paul's concern for his son and the whole family
17 crisis might have straightened him out for a while.
18
19 C&S has approximately sixty accountants who practice in three sections. The audit section
20 is the largest and most prestigious with approximately thirty accountants, less than a
21 third of whom are partners. Within the audit section, most accountants work on large,
22 lucrative accounts. Another important section is the tax section. They also do business
23 advice and estate work. I'm not sure exactly how many accountants they have. The firm
24 also has a small section devoted to small business matters. The idea behind this section
25 is that small businesses sometimes catch on and become very large businesses, and one
26 way to get their business is to have a group that pays attention to them when they are
27 small. That work was also an opportunity for training on cases where there was not as
28 much at stake and the fees charged were lower. They also have a group, not a formal
29 section, called accounting services. They provide accountants for audit clients that do not
30 have their own accounting staff.
31
32 As I said earlier, I was the deputy chair of the audit section of the firm from YR-5 for the
33 three years Paul was the chair. The chair chooses the deputy chair, so I started as deputy
34 solely at Paul Buckner's discretion. Our main functions were overseeing client-firm re-
35 lations and evaluating the performance of the accountants in our section of the firm,
36 in particular, the staff accountants as they progressed toward partnership. When Paul
37 stepped down as chair in September of YR-2, I continued to work as the deputy under the
38 current chair, Steve Ibanez, until I left the firm in April of YR-1.
39
40 The partnership decision at C&S is based on a series of performance evaluations of ac-
41 countants during their time with the firm. I can only speak with specificity about the audit
42 section's path from hiring to an offer of partnership. The firm normally hires ten or more
43 accountants who have passed the CPA exam for the audit section. Most of these will get
44 their CPA license, as required for partnership. The normal partnership track is seven to

1 nine years. In the history of the firm, there are two people, me and Alice Abraham in the
2 tax section of the firm, who made partner in six years. By the time the partnership deci-
3 sion is made, only three or four people from the beginning group of accountants are con-
4 sidered for partnership (the rest will have either been let go or decided to leave the firm).
5 At least 75 percent of the accountants who come forward for a partnership decision are
6 successful. The rest of the accountants leave the firm to other positions.
7
8 Each accountant's performance is evaluated every year, as close in time to the accoun-
9 tant's anniversary date as possible. Typically, because most accountants begin work in the
10 fall, most evaluations are in September or October. The C&S system is straightforward.
11 About a month before the evaluation, the chair and deputy chair of the audit section
12 identify the billable hours of the accountant, with a 2200-hour goal, together with those
13 payments collected from the client. The minimum acceptable collectables are 80 percent
14 or just under 1800. Each of those partners for whom significant work has been performed
15 is briefly interviewed and asked to evaluate the accountant's performance and to com-
16 ment on how the accountant's performance can improve. The rest of the partnership is
17 also solicited to provide any comments they have on any accountant. These are usually
18 made by phone or email. As the partnership decision gets closer, the ability of the ac-
19 countant to attract or maintain business is also an important factor. The chairman and
20 the deputy then amalgamate all the information and assign an evaluation of 1 to 5 to
21 the accountant's performance for the year. That amalgamation is kept in an electronic
22 employee file, which also contains other relevant information about the accountant. The
23 evaluations are set out in a series of yearly memos written by the chair of the section,
24 or the deputy, to the file of each accountant as they progress through the firm. Exhibits
25 3A–3G are the evaluation memos for Kiya Ahmed. Exhibits 5A–5H are the evaluation
26 memos for Mike DeAngelo—although I did not participate in his evaluation for YR-1, which
27 took place after I left the firm. The accountants are not shown the evaluation memo, but
28 they do receive a letter each year showing their raise in salary—a raise that is tied to the
29 evaluation. Exhibits 4A–4F are Kiya Ahmed's salary letters for her time with the firm.
30
31 The evaluation of 1 is reserved for the most extraordinary of performances; it is generally
32 not awarded until an accountant's fifth or sixth year. It is a clear indication the accountant
33 is likely to be offered a partnership sometime in the future. The evaluation of 2 is usually
34 the best evaluation accountants can receive in their first four years with the firm. It is a
35 sign the accountant is performing very well and is making good progress towards part-
36 nership, although partnership is not mentioned in evaluations until the fifth year. Only
37 about three to five staff accountants receive evaluations of 2 in their first through fourth
38 years. The evaluation of 2 in the fifth year and beyond is still considered excellent, but
39 generally connotes the accountant is borderline for partnership. An accountant will typi-
40 cally receive at least one evaluation of 1 before they are considered for partnership, and
41 most typically in the year in which they come up for partnership.
42
43 The evaluation of 3 is the typical evaluation received in the first two years of an accoun-
44 tant's career. It reflects a good, but not exemplary, performance. The evaluation of 3 in

1 years three and four is usually a good indicator the accountant will not make partner. Ac-
2 countants with an evaluation of 3 in their fourth year are typically advised to seek other
3 employment. In some cases, an accountant will be particularly bright and do very well in
4 analysis of accounting issues but lack the necessary communication and advocacy skills
5 to become a partner in the firm. In those cases, the accountant may be approached with
6 an offer of a permanent position as a senior accountant. Senior accountants have no
7 possibility of being made partners and are salaried employees of the firm paid at approxi-
8 mately the same level as a sixth-year accountant on the partnership track. An evaluation
9 of 3 in the fifth year is usually a clear sign the accountant will not make partner. With
10 some of these accountants, the firm will make efforts to place them in financial offices of
11 our good clients. Those positions pay very well and usually have excellent benefits. It is
12 the firm's interest to place former accountants with clients because it fosters good client
13 relations. In fact, I have several former C&S accountants working for me at NCW in the
14 CFO's office.
15
16 The evaluation of 4 is given for below expectation performance. While it is possible for
17 an accountant with an evaluation of 4 in the first year to improve and eventually go on
18 to partnership, a 4 in the first two years will usually result in a recommendation to seek
19 other employment. An evaluation of 4 in each of the first three years results in the setting
20 of a termination date, usually thirty days after the evaluation.
21
22 The evaluation of 5 is reserved for situations where the accountant has performed in an
23 incompetent manner. Because the firm is very careful in making hiring decisions, I know
24 of no accountant while I was there who ever received a 5 in an evaluation.
25
26 Once the evaluation has been assigned, the section chair, the deputy section chair, and
27 the accountant meet. The accountant is first given his or her evaluation for the year, then
28 the basis for the evaluation is explained. C&S never divulges the source of individual
29 partner comments to the accountant, but the nature of the comment often identifies its
30 source. During the meeting the section chair reads the amalgamation of the comments
31 that have been prepared by the chair and the deputy chair. If the accountant asks ques-
32 tions, the chair may refer to notes from interviews with individual partners, but that is
33 not the norm. The accountant is given an opportunity to comment on the evaluation or
34 ask questions. Finally, the accountant is told their raise for the next year. The accountant
35 does not receive any written evaluation.
36
37 The only record kept is the amalgamation of the comments from the partners and the
38 records on billable hours. Individual interview notes are destroyed after the evaluation
39 meeting. In addition, once an accountant is made a partner, the only records maintained
40 are those of the evaluations assigned for each year and their billable hours for each
41 year. Once an accountant leaves the firm, the records of evaluations and billable hours
42 are kept for approximately five or six years, in case the firm is contacted for a letter of
43 recommendation. The evaluation memos are destroyed once the accountant leaves the
44 firm. Exhibits 7A and 7B are a compilation of the records concerning the accountants

1 C&S hired in YR-9. It shows the billable hours and evaluations for each accountant in that
2 group during their time at C&S.
3
4 While the accountant does not get a copy of the evaluation record, they do receive, as
5 I said earlier, a written confirmation of their raise. Raises are based on a set formula that
6 coincides with the evaluation the accountant has received. The raise scale is as follows:
7 1–7 percent; 2–5 percent; 3–3 percent; and 4–2 percent. Salaries are also adjusted peri-
8 odically to reflect increases in base salary. These increases are irrespective of merit and
9 are reflected on the salary letters as market adjustments.
10
11 Partnership decisions are usually made in June of the seventh year of an accountant's
12 tenure with the firm. An accountant may ask for a partnership review in their sixth year,
13 but if such a request is made and partnership is denied, the decision is final. In addition,
14 in unusual cases, an accountant may extend their partnership track to a decision as late
15 as their ninth year. For an accountant to be made a partner, the accountant must be nom-
16 inated by the partners in their section. The nomination is by majority vote. That nomina-
17 tion goes to the firm's executive committee. The executive committee then recommends
18 the accountant to the entire partnership. The executive committee normally implements
19 the recommendations of the three sections of the firm (audit, tax, and small business)
20 unless in the committee's opinion a particular section is too top-heavy with partners.
21 During my time at the firm, I know of no occasion when the executive committee has not
22 recommended for partnership an accountant who has been nominated by their section,
23 although I believe there was one circumstance where the executive committee made an
24 accountant wait a year before they were recommended to the entire partnership. The
25 recommendation of the executive committee is then voted on by all partners. A majority
26 vote is required to achieve partnership. It is very unusual for the entire partnership to
27 vote down an accountant who has been recommended by both his or her section and the
28 executive committee. During my time at C&S that only happened twice.
29
30 Kiya Ahmed came to work as a staff assistant at the firm at about the same time that
31 I started as a staff accountant. I didn't have very much to do with her until YR-15, when
32 she was assigned to work one of Paul Buckner's engagements to which I was also as-
33 signed. This engagement involved a dispute among the largest banks in the state of Nita.
34 It was extremely complex and involved difficult accounting issues. It was the engagement
35 in which Paul Buckner established himself as one of the best, if not the best, accounting
36 expert witnesses in the firm, and probably in the city as well. (Of course, now he enjoys
37 a national reputation for excellence in audit litigation support.) Kiya was chosen to work
38 as one of the staff assistants when the case came to trial in January of YR-13. As a fourth-
39 year CPA, I was assigned as managing staff accountant. My duties were to coordinate
40 between the two partners who were working on accounting issues and supporting the
41 lawyers who were trying the case and the staff assistants from our firm assigned to the
42 case. During that trial, Kiya and I worked quite closely together. I was impressed with her
43 intellect and how quickly she assimilated and understood directions given to her and an-
44 ticipated other needs in the trial. Paul Buckner was also impressed with Kiya's work. He

1   encouraged her to apply to graduate school to get an MBA degree, which she did. Since
2   she was applying to Nita University, as an alumnus I volunteered to write a recommenda-
3   tion letter for her.
4
5   Kiya was accepted to Nita University for the online MBA program. The Nita University
6   program has a good reputation among online schools, with courses taught by full-time
7   faculty or senior practicing accountants. The education available was considered to be
8   roughly equal to the full-time MBA program, with a little less deep-dive theory and a little
9   more hands-on practical education. Kiya had to enroll in the online program because she
10   was a single mother of small children and needed to support them while she attended
11   school. She continued to work as a staff assistant at C&S during her first year of graduate
12   school. She did very well in school, and we offered her a position as a senior staff assis-
13   tant with the firm, which meant a pay raise for her. During her three years of graduate
14   school, Kiya frequently worked for me. She was bright, insightful, and talented. I called
15   Paul's attention to her work from time to time and kept him posted on Kiya's successes
16   in graduate school. He complimented her work, as did I—but I know compliments com-
17   ing from a star like Paul Buckner meant more to her. She graduated summa cum laude,
18   finished first in her class, and was recognized for research and writing work she did on
19   publication projects of a couple of her professors; all while working full time at C&S and
20   having the responsibilities of a single mother.
21
22   As you can tell I was, and am, quite a fan of Kiya Ahmed. In the early fall of her third and
23   final year of graduate school, unbeknownst to her, I went to Paul Buckner and spoke
24   on Kiya's behalf about her getting a position as a staff accountant with C&S. Although
25   Paul didn't embrace the idea immediately, he thought it worth checking out with the
26   hiring committee. C&S had never hired one of its staff assistants as a staff accountant,
27   as a matter of policy, and had never hired a graduate of any online program as a staff
28   accountant. That policy was based on a misconception that the online program is some-
29   how different than the regular in-class program in quality of education, which is not ac-
30   curate. Not hiring staff assistants made sense as a matter of policy in that it minimized
31   competition among the staff assistants, avoiding interference with productivity. Not
32   hiring graduates of Nita University's online program (or any online program) made no
33   sense at all.
34
35   Paul and I quietly circulated the idea around the hiring committee, of which I was a mem-
36   ber and Paul was the chair. Most people on the committee seemed amenable to recruit-
37   ing Kiya.
38
39   We approached Kiya with the idea of applying to C&S and she seemed genuinely flat-
40   tered. She applied and went through the formal interviewing process. Kiya sailed through
41   the preliminary interviews and was invited to a full day of interviews. She did quite well.
42   We already knew the high quality of her work, as supported by Paul Buckner, who was
43   known in the firm as being very demanding. In many ways Kiya was a much more certain
44   product than someone who had never worked in the firm.

1   The only major stumbling block was Kiya's requirement that she not be assigned to any
2   engagements that took her out of Nita City for extended periods of time—a necessity
3   because she was a single parent. C&S had and has a regional practice, which is quite a big
4   area, and a few of our partners (like Paul Buckner) had national reputations that broad-
5   ened their geographical reach. This requirement limited the range of matters on which
6   Kiya could work, and this caused problems with several of my partners, the most vocal
7   of whom was Danielle Reddick. This seemed odd, in that Danielle worked exclusively on
8   small business matters that were almost always local in nature, but her complaint did
9   have some merit. Paul and I argued on Kiya's behalf—there was plenty of work of vary-
10 ing complexity in and around Nita City, and the children would eventually grow up and
11 be more independent. That argument, and Kiya's talent, carried the day. Some questions
12 were asked about the quality of the education in the online program at Nita University,
13 but I was able to answer those questions sufficiently to remove that as an impediment.
14
15 The committee voted to offer Kiya a position as a staff accountant. Paul Buckner made
16 the offer personally and Kiya accepted. She later thanked me for all my help and told me
17 she would prove that our confidence in her was deserved. Kiya came to see me in July of
18 YR-9 when she received the formal letter from the firm that set her salary. She was con-
19 cerned that the language of the letter did not indicate that she would not be required to
20 travel extensively, despite the clear understanding she had with the firm. (See Exhibit 2.)
21 I assured her that the firm was well aware of her special requirements and not to worry
22 about the letter; it was just a form letter.
23
24 Our confidence in Kiya was well placed. She passed all four sections of her CPA exam on
25 her first attempt (something not accomplished by many of our hires), and when the Nita
26 CPA Board accepted Kiya's accounting work with C&S as her apprenticeship year, she be-
27 came a licensed CPA immediately.
28
29 I became a mentor of sorts for Kiya Ahmed. I knew how important Paul's guidance had
30 been for me as I worked myself up through the firm to partnership; I thought I could give
31 Kiya similar guidance. I felt a special responsibility towards her because I had recruited
32 her to the firm and because she graduated from my school. I knew the added pressure
33 on an accountant who was the first from a school to work at the firm, or in her case, the
34 first from the online program at Nita University—I felt it when I was the first accountant
35 from the Nita University at C&S. I liked Kiya as a person and admired how she had worked
36 her way through school while being a single mother.
37
38 I talked up Kiya to my partners so they would request her to work on various projects.
39 I was confident that, with the right opportunities, Kiya would flourish at the firm. I also
40 warned her to avoid being pigeonholed in less-desirable specialties within the firm. The
41 accountants in the audit section of the firm work on the full range of problems faced by
42 their large corporate clients, and the second largest group, Tax/Business Planning, work
43 a wide variety of issues for the corporate clients. But a smaller group headed by Danielle
44 Reddick services smaller clients as a loss-leader. The hope is that some of these smaller

1   clients will flourish and remain loyal to the firm as they need more and more sophisticated
2   services. This proved true in several circumstances, and Danielle's group has grown. But
3   it still lacks the prestige of Audit and Tax. While I was with the firm, it was much harder
4   to become a partner in the Audit and Tax groups. That's where the top talent wanted to
5   be, and the partnership slots were limited. In tax or audit, the accountants work with a
6   broader range of clients; the firm regards that work as having greater complexity and re-
7   quiring higher analytical skills. These perceptions may have been inaccurate, but because
8   they existed, they might as well have been real. The one concrete reality, though, was
9   that tax and audit billed at a higher rate than the small business group.
10
11 It was generally perceived in the firm to be easier to become a partner in the small
12 business group because Danielle argued she needed partners to service small business
13 owners who did not want to be relegated to lesser-credentialed staff and because the
14 partners in her group were almost always compensated in relation to the returns of her
15 group, so the firm did not bear any extra burden from making partners of Danielle's can-
16 didates. Also, the small business group almost always had a higher percentage return on
17 collectibles. The group's clients had smaller bills and nearly always paid on time. Danielle
18 was very good at weeding out the non-payers very quickly. The small business group was
19 a particularly bad choice for women accountants because many of the older members of
20 the firm (virtually all men) viewed that practice with disdain, referring to it in a deroga-
21 tory way as "light service work." Now that you ask, it's true that for most of the time I was
22 with the firm, the only women partners were in this area.
23
24 I did my best to guide Kiya through the political minefields of the firm, and she seemed
25 grateful for my help. She also followed my advice most of the time, and through the first
26 four years of her practice at C&S she did quite well. She received good assignments, and
27 she impressed most of the partners for whom she worked. She worked for me on several
28 engagements in that period and did terrific work. There was some mild criticism of her
29 writing in her first year, but that was typical of almost all our accountants. She was evalu-
30 ated at a 3 in her first year, which put her in the top half of accountants at her experience
31 level. I recall she was upset with her evaluation, but I told her not to be; the evaluation
32 was typical and if she kept doing good work she would be fine.
33
34 In Kiya's second-, third-, and fourth-year evaluations, she received a 2, which I believe put
35 her in the top three or four of accountants at her level. Her evaluations were uniformly
36 good, and she was in demand from other partners. What lobbying I did for her focused
37 on encouraging the most senior partners to give her assignments because they held so
38 much influence in partnership decisions. There were very few negative comments. A cou-
39 ple of the old-timers at the firm would, from time to time, complain about her not being
40 "aggressive" or "tough" enough, which I believe was a code for "she's a woman," but
41 those comments should not have been taken seriously, and I told Kiya as much. In addi-
42 tion, there was one offensive email sent during Kiya's fourth-year review by an obviously
43 racist audit partner, referring to Kiya's ethnicity, calling her a terrorist who might frighten
44 our audit clients and he didn't want our clients seeing one of our professionals in a burka.

1   After consulting with Paul, I immediately emailed the partner back, condemning his email
2   in no uncertain terms, and informing him that his views did not in any way express the
3   policy or attitude of the firm. I believe we saved those emails as part of Kiya's file in her
4   fourth-year evaluation. In fact, Kiya, did not wear a burka. She did wear a headscarf com-
5   ing and going from the office, but did not wear her headscarf while working either in the
6   firm or at the offices of clients. In fact, I am unaware of any other negative comment by
7   anyone about Kiya's ethnicity (her parents are U.S. citizens who emigrated from Egypt)
8   nor her Muslim religion. Unknown to the idiot partner who wrote the email, apparently
9   there are at least two Muslims, both male, who are partners in the firm.

10

11 The one negative comment that had some substance came from Danielle Reddick who
12 felt it was inappropriate for Kiya to confine her practice to engagements that kept her
13 in Nita City, or at least required minimum time out of town. Danielle felt Kiya's lack of
14 travel burdened other accountants and kept the firm from evaluating how Kiya per-
15 formed with the added stress of working in unfamiliar places and dealing with unfamil-
16 iar client business structures. She felt this evaluation was important because so much
17 of C&S's practice was outside of Nita City, and if Kiya made partner she would be ex-
18 pected to travel where her engagements took her. When I reminded Danielle that the
19 travel issue had been raised, discussed, and decided when Kiya was interviewing with
20 the firm, her response was that the children had to be old enough by now to deal with
21 childcare help in the home when Kiya was required to travel. Danielle's was the only
22 such comment, nothing really came of it, and later Kiya did start working on out of town
23 engagements.

24

25 Kiya had a terrible fifth year as an accountant, and it could not have come at a worse
26 time. By the time an accountant is in her fifth year, the partners take a very close look
27 at her performance. This is because by this point the accountant is fully trained and is
28 dealing with relatively complex factual settings involving difficult analytical issues. As a
29 result, the fifth year usually provides an excellent marker for partnership potential. Kiya's
30 terrible year, however, was not a reflection of her abilities, but caused by a series of per-
31 sonal problems.

32

33 As I understand it, both of Kiya's children, who were teenagers at the time, went through
34 difficult periods, while at the same time her father was diagnosed with cancer and died.
35 The coincidence of these events kept Kiya from focusing on her work. Her billable hours
36 dipped significantly, and the quality of her work diminished as well. Because I was aware
37 of her personal situation, I covered for her on the work she did for me, but other partners
38 were less generous in evaluating her work product, and fairly so. This was even though
39 they were aware of Kiya's personal problems. Their complaint was that at C&S the pres-
40 sure of the practice and the need to perform at a high level does not diminish because
41 an accountant has personal problems. They expressed concern that a pattern of such
42 behavior at the onset of personal crises would develop, and that was a problem. I was
43 privy to these comments because by that time, in YR-4, Paul Buckner was chair of the
44 audit section, and I was his deputy.

1 Kiya's evaluation was a 3 for the year. The partners in the audit section authorized Paul
2 to use his influence to place her in the financial office of one of our client companies
3 or agree to give her a strong recommendation should she choose to seek alternative
4 employment herself. Some of the partners in the section felt those should be Kiya's only
5 two options. Mainly because of my faith in Kiya and her ability, and at my insistence, Paul
6 persuaded the audit partners that Kiya should be given a shot at redeeming herself by
7 working on a very important antitrust engagement of his that was heating up for one of
8 our best clients, Nita Computer World (NCW). If it had not been for Paul Buckner, Kiya's
9 career with C&S would have ended in YR-4. That's why what happened to Kiya later was
10 so ironic.
11
12 Paul and I presented Kiya with her evaluation and with the options available to her. Al-
13 though she was disappointed with her evaluation, she opted to work on the NCW engage-
14 ment, as I knew she would. No one doubted Kiya Ahmed's commitment and ambition to
15 be one of the best.
16
17 I was not involved in the NCW antitrust engagement, but I got periodic reports from Paul
18 on Kiya's performance. As I predicted, she performed magnificently, according to Paul,
19 and he complimented me on my judgment. I had a conversation with Paul Buckner about
20 Kiya Ahmed's work on NCW. He confirmed she was still doing a great job and asked what
21 I knew about Kiya's personal life. I told him about her children, but I knew he was aware
22 of them and the problems Kiya had with them the previous year. He asked if she was in-
23 volved with anyone romantically, and I said I didn't know. It was obvious Paul's interest in
24 Kiya went beyond the professional.
25
26 For some reason I felt very protective towards Kiya. I told Paul that if he was interested
27 in her, other than as an accountant, that he had better be serious, because I felt she was
28 very vulnerable at the time. I asked him not to take advantage of her. Paul smiled and
29 asked me whether there was anything going on between Kiya and me. I, of course, told
30 him there wasn't. He said I shouldn't worry about Kiya; she was a big girl and could han-
31 dle herself. He told me not to worry, he would "be gentle." I must have visibly bristled,
32 because he said, "Don't worry, everything will work out fine." Paul then moved on to
33 other matters involving the audit section administration, signaling that the conversation
34 about Kiya was over.
35
36 During the early spring of YR-3, it became obvious to me that a personal relationship
37 was developing between Kiya and Paul. They were always out of town together on the
38 NCW engagement, and they were inseparable when they were in the office. The rumors
39 of another Paul Buckner affair buzzed around the office, and although I wasn't certain
40 anything was going on, the signs were all there.
41
42 At the same time, the NCW engagement was progressing very well and, according to
43 Paul, Kiya had performed brilliantly. When the case settled on extremely favorable terms
44 to NCW in June of YR-3, the client was so happy they invited the entire litigation team

1 and spouses to a week's vacation in the Bahamas at the client's expense. It was at this
2 vacation that the affair between Paul and Kiya became public knowledge within the firm.
3 According to others from the firm, Kiya and Paul were in each other's company con-
4 stantly, from the earliest in the morning until the latest at night. They were also seen
5 strolling arm in arm on the beach. When they returned, their relationship was obvious
6 to everyone.
7
8 Given Paul's history, I felt it was my responsibility as Kiya's friend and mentor to counsel
9 her about the risks of her relationship with Paul Buckner. I asked Kiya whether she was
10 aware of Paul's history with other women at the firm and she told me she was. She told
11 me this time it was different; Paul was going to leave his wife once his youngest son
12 went away to college. I responded by saying something like "he's said that before," and
13 Kiya told me she didn't want to discuss the matter any further. I said I hoped everything
14 worked out for her but, if it didn't, I didn't think I could protect her interests at the firm.
15 She looked sort of stunned, but just said thanks for my concern and I left. My statement
16 to her was meant to convey the risk to her future at the firm if her continued employ-
17 ment was viewed as contrary to Paul Buckner's wishes. I can't say Paul ever personally
18 got an accountant or staff assistant with whom he was romantically involved dismissed
19 from the firm, but I do believe my partners would do whatever they thought necessary
20 to keep Paul Buckner happy. After all, he was a major source of business for the firm—
21 one of our few nationally acclaimed members—and we couldn't afford to lose him. Also,
22 I know of no woman at the firm who survived there after an affair with Paul Buckner.
23
24 Because of the work Kiya had done on NCW, as reported effusively by Paul Buckner,
25 and maybe because some of the lower level partners wanted to get on Paul's good side,
26 Kiya was very much in demand for high-quality assignments during the summer of YR-3.
27 She apparently performed very well because she received glowing reports during her
28 sixth-year evaluation process. In addition, the general counsel at NCW wrote a letter con-
29 gratulating the entire litigation team, giving special praise to Kiya. (See Exhibit 6.) Several
30 of the other partners in the audit section even congratulated me on my good judgment
31 in backing Kiya so strongly the previous year. Because of the high praise for her work and
32 enormous number of billable hours, virtually all collectable, Kiya received a 1 evaluation
33 for her sixth year—a strong, positive indicator for a favorable partnership decision in the
34 seventh year. When Paul and I informed Kiya of her evaluation, she was ecstatic. Paul
35 came around the desk and gave her a big hug and a kiss. Kiya looked embarrassed that
36 Paul did that when I was in the room, so I just congratulated her and went back to my
37 office.
38
39 During the fall of YR-3, Kiya was assigned to work on another engagement for NCW on
40 which I was the lead partner. It was nowhere near as complex as the one the previous
41 year, but it did give her another chance to show her talent. It involved a similar trade
42 secrets protection issue as the previous NCW engagement that Kiya handled. She took
43 good advantage of the opportunity and performed very well, at least during the fall of
44 YR-3.

1   In the early part of YR-2, the inevitable happened and Paul Buckner ended his affair with
2   Kiya Ahmed. Kiya went into a deep depression. For the next several months her work
3   was off, and she seemed to be constantly suffering from a cold or the flu. As a result, the
4   requests for her to work on engagements also dropped off. It's possible the drop-off in
5   work requests was also a result of Kiya's breakup with Paul. Just as some partners might
6   try to curry favor with Paul by asking for Kiya when they knew she was involved with
7   him, the opposite might also be true. I do not believe Paul Buckner was directly respon-
8   sible for the drop-off in Kiya's assignments in that I never heard anyone say Paul had ap-
9   proached them, but as I said, my partners might have reacted to what they thought Paul
10   wanted. I just don't know.

11

12   At any rate, when I collected information for a partnership vote by the audit section
13   on the four people eligible for partnership that year, I received some negative evalu-
14   ations of Kiya's work. I also noted that her billable hours were sharply lower. She had
15   billed 850 hours for September YR-3 through January YR-2 and only 550 hours for the
16   four months leading up to her evaluation. In addition, I heard questions again about
17   her toughness and resiliency, and her ability to not let personal matters interfere
18   with her work. There were even some questions raised about her intellectual abil-
19   ity, which I hadn't heard since Kiya's first year with the firm. And even though the
20   NCW engagement should have answered any questions about how she performed
21   when in unfamiliar settings, those criticisms also resurfaced, especially from Danielle
22   Reddick.

23

24   I can't prove Paul Buckner did or said anything overtly about Kiya that caused the nega-
25   tive evaluations. He really wouldn't need to. Their breakup was public information and
26   some of my colleagues might have evaluated Kiya negatively to try to please Paul. The
27   breakup could certainly explain her drop-off in assignments as many of my partners
28   wouldn't want to appear to favor Kiya over Paul.

29

30   I approached Kiya with the bad news I was receiving. While I was not specific, I gave her
31   the gist of the negative comments. I also noted the sharp drop-off in billable hours. Kiya
32   said she just hadn't gotten a lot of assignments. I asked her why she hadn't come to me,
33   and she said she really didn't think anything of it at the time; she thought it was just a
34   down work cycle. I wish she had said something, or I had been more attentive. Lack of
35   billables became a strong issue for Kiya's opponents, as it and collectables are the only
36   objective indicia of the value of an accountant to the firm. I gave her my best advice and
37   told her that in my opinion it was not a good idea to push for partnership that year. I did
38   tell her that, if she chose to go forward, I would support her nomination for partnership
39   by the audit section, but she would be in a much better position if she waited a year and
40   repeated her sixth-year performance. I assured her I would make certain she got the right
41   assignments to showcase her talents. She didn't speak right away, and when she did,
42   she asked whether Paul Buckner had anything to do with her negative evaluation. When
43   I didn't answer immediately, she just said, "Never mind, I'll get back to you in a couple of
44   days," and I left her office.

1   Several days later Kiya came by my office and told me she wanted to go forward with a
2   decision that year. I again tried to talk her out of it, but her mind was made up, so I told
3   her I'd do what she wished; she had my support. Paul had asked me to prepare Kiya's
4   evaluation, which I did. Her evaluation was really in two parts. Her work was excellent
5   during the fall and then fell off in the winter and spring. As a result, I evaluated her at the
6   2 level.

7

8   The four people up for partnership nomination that year from the audit section were
9   Roger Kramer, Mark Hancock, Michael DeAngelo, and Kiya. The meeting began on a Thurs-
10   day afternoon with a consideration of Michael DeAngelo. Mike had consistently been
11   evaluated at the 2 level in his evaluations. Although not regarded as a superstar, he was
12   considered as a rock-solid performer with uniformly good skills. There was some question
13   about his ability to attract business and about how he did on client relations. The question
14   about client relations hung up the partners and we went round and round on the matter.
15   There was also the usual argument about whether being solid is enough, especially in a
16   year when there were other candidates for partnership who had all scored at the 1 level,
17   at least for one year. In the end, the partners sent me back to Mike with a suggestion that
18   he hold off for another year. The next year's class was not nearly so strong, and it would
19   also give Mike another year to improve his evaluation. Although reluctant, Mike accepted
20   the recommendation and withdrew for consideration in YR-2. This was a very good move
21   on his part as the reports on Mike's performance for the second half of YR-2 were ter-
22   rific and continued through YR-1. In addition, he attracted a good-sized client to the firm.
23   I understand he received a partnership offer in June of YR-1.

24

25   Mark Hancock was an easy case. He too consistently received solid 2 evaluations, and
26   although not brilliant was a solid performer. What distinguished Mark was his analytical
27   ability. During the spring of YR-2, he produced a devastating analysis of the prior writ-
28   ings and deposition testimony of two opposing expert witnesses. His mentor credited
29   him for winning the case in a very important interference with contract matter for one
30   of our best clients. His performance rated him a 1 for his seventh year, and the client's
31   insistence on his being on future audit teams made him a lock for partnership. He was
32   nominated after a brief discussion, which mostly praised his abilities.

33

34   Roger Kramer was next and he, too, was an easy case. Roger was generally considered
35   one of the smartest accountants in the firm. He had received evaluations at the 1 level in
36   both his fifth and sixth years. Roger was also very personable and did very well with the
37   clients on whose engagements he worked. He was also the son of the president of one
38   of our better clients, who we felt we would certainly lose if Roger was at a comparable
39   firm. His billable hours were good but not exceptional; if he had a weakness, it was in that
40   area. The only real question with Roger was whether he should have received a partner-
41   ship offer in his sixth year. As expected, Roger breezed through.

42

43   The meeting then adjourned until Friday afternoon for the consideration of Kiya's candi-
44   dacy. The meeting began at approximately 3:00 p.m. and lasted until 8:00 p.m. Kiya had

1 several very strong supporters, including myself, who thought she possessed a great com-
2 bination of skills and she would do great work on anything to which she was assigned.
3 Her detractors raised all the issues I mentioned before, Danielle Reddick being one of the
4 most vociferous, and the debate was long and rancorous. Paul Buckner, who chaired the
5 meeting as chair of the audit section, spoke very little. He did speak about Kiya's work
6 on the NCW case in glowing terms, but admitted that Kiya's performance in YR-2 was
7 troublesome. As chair of the section, he was not required to vote, but announced that
8 he was going to abstain in the vote. His abstention, in my opinion, was the equivalent
9 of a negative vote and probably was one of the determining factors in the outcome. In
10 the end, however, the feeling that Kiya had been inconsistent in her performance, in the
11 view of some, reflected a lack of toughness and resiliency, plus the fact that she was not
12 able to attract any business to the firm, carried the day. In a close vote, her nomination
13 for partnership was denied. I tried to get the partnership to allow her another year to
14 improve her performance, but the audit partners seemed to not have the stomach for a
15 repeat of that meeting in a year. I was told to inform Kiya that she had six months to find
16 another position.
17
18 I found Kiya in her office when the meeting ended. She took the news hard. She asked if
19 she could have another year to improve, but I told her the decision was final. She asked
20 what Paul's position at the meeting was, and I told her I couldn't divulge individual com-
21 ments as a matter of policy. I told her I was sorry; I had done my best, but that there was
22 nothing I could do.
23
24 After the meeting, I ran into Paul Buckner outside his office. He invited me in for a drink.
25 He asked if I had talked with Kiya and I told him I had, and she had taken the news pretty
26 hard. He knew Kiya was a favorite of mine, and he asked how I was doing. Something
27 snapped, and I lit into him. I told him he was an egomaniac and if he had exercised a little
28 control of his libido that Kiya would be a partner today. I told him he was a real jerk and
29 he had ruined a terrific career. Paul looked shocked. I had never talked to him that way
30 before. He didn't deny my accusation, but he did say it was Kiya who had ended the rela-
31 tionship, not him, and he was sorry about how it had worked out. He said he knew how
32 I felt about Kiya and again said he was sorry, but this time to me. I told Paul I would draft
33 Kiya's recommendation letter for him, to help her secure a new position. He said that was
34 fine. I got up and walked out of Paul's office.
35
36 Ever since that day my relationship with Paul Buckner has been different. Although we
37 still interacted on business matters in a professional manner, the closeness we once had
38 was gone. To be honest, I lost some respect for him. I think the same was true firmwide,
39 because in September of YR-2, Paul was replaced as the chief of the audit section after
40 only three years in the position. The normal term for that position is five years. When
41 the Executive Committee announced the change in leadership, it was couched in an ex-
42 planation that Paul's work schedule was too demanding to allow him sufficient time to
43 administer the section, but the gossip in the firm is that the whole situation with Kiya was
44 the straw that broke the camel's back as far as tolerance for Paul's dalliances. The new

1 chief of the division is Steve Ibanez. He asked me to stay on as deputy for purposes of
2 continuity, and I agreed to do so.
3
4 Kiya did not handle her firing well. Although she interviewed for jobs with other firms,
5 nothing came of it. Originally, I thought her confidence had been undermined by the
6 whole episode at C&S, and that probably affected her interviewing skills. I now know
7 of a couple of circumstances when Paul Buckner did her in with a poor reference letter.
8 I only found out about the letters in January of YR-1. Kiya called to tell me she had a copy
9 the letter Paul wrote to John Randall of the Morrison firm in Nita City, which was far from
10 complimentary. She read the letter to me, including some handwritten comments I now
11 recognize to be in Paul's handwriting. (See Exhibit 11.) I felt terrible about this because
12 I had given Kiya a copy of the letter I had drafted for Paul's signature and had encouraged
13 her to use him as a reference. (See Exhibit 10.) He had never been vindictive after any
14 previous affair, so I was really surprised that he was with Kiya. When I confronted him
15 with the fact that he didn't use my letter, Paul became very defensive and told me to
16 mind my own business. I lost what respect I had for Paul personally, although I have to
17 concede to him his accounting abilities.
18
19 I learned Kiya was looking for a teaching job. I offered to help her out financially with
20 whatever kind of loan she needed. She turned down my offer. Eventually Kiya ended up
21 with teaching offers from both Nita University and Conwell University, although it took a
22 while for them to come in. I'm happy to say she returned to our alma mater, where I'm
23 sure she will be a great success.
24
25 I also know she filed a complaint against the firm with the EEOC. The firm received
26 notice of her allegations in the summer of YR-2. (See Exhibit 14.) As the deputy of the
27 audit section, I was contacted to be sure to maintain whatever files we still had on
28 Kiya and the other people who came up for partner in YR-2. We had the paragraph
29 evaluations on Kiya and Mike DeAngelo because they were still accountants at the time
30 the firm received the EEOC letter. Because Mark Hancock and Roger Kramer had been
31 made partners by that time, the only records we had on them for their years as non-
32 partners were their evaluations and their billable hours. The same was true of former
33 accountants with Kiya's level of experience who had left the firm. (See Exhibits 7A and
34 7B.) The firm returned the EEOC notice with a general denial written by our attorneys
35 and signed by our chair, Robert Bryant. (See Exhibit 15.) Sometime in early January
36 of YR-1 we received a copy of the "right to sue" letter the EEOC had sent to Kiya.
37 (See Exhibit 16.)
38
39 Kiya resigned in December of YR-2 when her six-month grace period with the firm ended.
40 I asked if there was anything I could do, and she told me no; she thought everything
41 would work out. As I said, I told her if she needed a loan I was always available. She
42 thanked me but said she didn't think that would be necessary. I told her I was aware of
43 her complaint to the EEOC and said I would be willing to testify on her behalf if the need
44 ever arose. She gave me a hug and left the firm.

1   The whole matter with Kiya Ahmed left a sour taste in my mouth for the politics of C&S,
2   so when NCW approached me about my current job, I pursued the opportunity. I was
3   surprised it was so easy for me to leave C&S, but I guess the time was right. I have a ter-
4   rific job at NCW. I am the vice president for financial matters and the CFO. I oversee the
5   entire financial operation and our small legal department. Our audit work is farmed out
6   to C&S. Paul Buckner still handles our most important matters and I interact with him
7   professionally, but we have no personal relationship any longer. I have not talked to him
8   about Kiya's lawsuit against the firm, nor have I talked with C&S's lawyers.
9
10 When I got the job at NCW, one of the first people I tried to hire into our finance depart-
11 ment was Kiya Ahmed. At the time I offered her the job, with a starting salary of $95,000,
12 in May of YR-1, she had already accepted the teaching position at Nita University Law
13 School as a practice professor, so she turned me down. I told her there would always be
14 a position for her at NCW if she ever changed her mind. Kiya and I continue to see each
15 other socially from time to time. We are good friends. I'll have to admit, because you've
16 asked, that I would be interested in a romantic relationship with her, but we have never
17 interacted in that way, and I don't expect we ever will.

I have read this deposition and it is complete and accurate.

Bill Weisman
Bill Weisman

Subscribed and sworn before me this 9th day of July, YR-0.

Harry Gibbons
Harry Gibbons
Certified Shorthand Reporter

This deposition was taken in the office of the counsel for the defendants on June 24th,
YR-0. This deposition was given under oath and was read and signed by the deponent.

STATEMENT OF RACHEL LEVIN

1   My name is Rachel Levin. I am forty-five years old and live at 212 West Woolsey Way in
2   Nita City with my husband, David. Our children Greg and Melissa, who are twins, are
3   second-year law students at Nita University School of Law here in Nita City. David is an
4   Assistant United States Attorney in the civil division. I work in the accounting firm of
5   Anderson & Jones as an office manager for the audit portion of the practice. I have been
6   working at Anderson & Jones since YR-4. I have a bachelor's degree in business admin-
7   istration from Nita State University, which I received in YR-24. I began work at the Nita
8   Stock Exchange that year but left in YR-23 when my twins were born. I stayed out of the
9   job market until YR-15, when the twins were in the second grade.
10
11   At that time, I accepted a job offer from an old friend of the family, Charles Milton, to
12   come work for him at the accounting firm of Cooper & Stewart. Charles persuaded me to
13   work for him as his staff assistant. Although I had no experience working in an accounting
14   firm, I had been around accountants all my life. My mom graduated from Nita University
15   and she worked as an accountant for the U.S. Attorney's Office until she retired in YR-3.
16   She introduced me to my husband, who was a clerk for one of the federal judges at the
17   time we met. My dad was an economics professor at Nita University. He also retired in
18   YR-3, and my parents now live in Lake Worth, Florida.
19
20   My job for Mr. Milton was as an administrative assistant. He was head of the audit
21   practice at the firm, so my responsibilities included supervising his clerical and other
22   administrative work, maintaining his calendar, and scheduling all his engagements, meet-
23   ings, travel arrangements, etc. I also handled communication between Mr. Milton and
24   other partners, senior accountants, and staff accountants, as well as staff assistants who
25   worked on his engagements. Mr. Milton was a contemporary of my parents. He went to
26   undergraduate school with them, and they remained friends while he was in his MBA
27   program. He was in his mid- to late-fifties when I went to work for him. He was a senior
28   partner at C&S and was involved in numerous engagements, but probably spent most of
29   his time in attracting and keeping clients for the firm. As a result, I also was responsible
30   for maintaining his active business and social schedule.
31
32   Earlier this year, my son was home for dinner on Sunday and mentioned that he thought
33   his Accounting for Lawyers elective second-year course's professor was a terrific teacher.
34   He also said that according to her bio she had worked at Cooper & Stewart during the
35   time I was there. He said the professor's name was Professor Ahmed. It turned out his
36   professor was Kiya Ahmed, who I remembered from my time at C&S.
37
38   When Ms. Ahmed was a staff accountant, Charles Milton was the chair of the audit sec-
39   tion of the firm. As part of his job he was responsible for accumulating information and
40   then evaluating each accountant in the section on a yearly basis. I recall Ms. Ahmed
41   from that process, mainly because during one of her evaluations, she challenged one of
42   the evaluations she received from a partner, and she had several meetings with Charles

1   about the evaluation. I don't remember which evaluation it was, but it would have
2   been in the time Charles was the chair of the audit section. I also recall Charles used
3   Ms. Ahmed's services on several engagements after that, and she had done quite well for
4   him, but I can't recall any of the specifics.
5
6   I told all of this to Greg, and he told me the word at law school was that C&S fired Profes-
7   sor Ahmed because she wouldn't have sex with one of the partners, that they discrimi-
8   nated against her because she was a Muslim, and that she had sued the firm. He asked
9   me what kind of place I worked for because he was sure Professor Ahmed was in the
10   right. I told Greg that as far as I knew the only partner capable of such activity was Paul
11   Buckner. Buckner had a reputation as a real sexual predator in the firm and his antics
12   were well known. Even though he was a married man with several children, a week didn't
13   go by that there wasn't a rumor about him going after some young woman at the firm.
14   I told Greg I had never heard anybody say anything negative about Muslims, though, and
15   I believed several of the partners were Muslim.
16
17   I know for a fact that about ten years ago Buckner forced a fine young woman out
18   of the firm. Her name was Carol Merritt. Carol was a young accountant at the time.
19   She was married to a nice young man. I met her when she came to meet with Charles
20   about work she was doing for him. I met her husband at a party celebrating a big
21   win in one of Charles's battles with a federal government agency on which she was
22   a member of the audit team. He seemed like a nice guy. I remember having a long
23   conversation with Carol and her husband at the party. Unlike some accountants, who
24   wouldn't waste their time with someone other than a partner at such a gathering,
25   Carol and her husband were most cordial to me and my husband. We talked about a
26   variety of things, including David's and my mom's experiences at the U.S. Attorney's
27   Office.
28
29   After that, Carol stopped by to say hello when her work brought her to Charles's office
30   or the nearby office of another partner. She did some other work for Charles, but I can't
31   recall anything specific about how she did on those engagements. I know about Carol's
32   affair with Buckner. It was common knowledge in the firm.
33
34   Buckner apparently swept Carol off her feet and persuaded her to leave her husband and
35   move into an apartment I'm sure Buckner paid for. It was obvious Carol was uncomfort-
36   able with the situation, but I guess she didn't know how to turn Buckner down.
37
38   At some point, I don't know exactly when or how, Buckner dumped Carol and she fell re-
39   ally hard. Fortunately, her husband took her back. It was obvious he truly loved her. But
40   Carol never returned to the firm. It was common knowledge Buckner didn't like to have
41   his former conquests around the firm. I don't have any specific information about this,
42   but that was the word around the firm. I can't remember any of their names, but several
43   times I heard that women accountants or staff assistants whom Buckner preyed on were
44   forced out of the firm after he no longer had any use for them.

1   I never saw or heard from Carol after that. I know Charles wrote several letters on her be-
2   half to firms in Washington, DC, where she and her husband moved. I remember Charles
3   saying he felt somewhat responsible for what happened to Carol because Charles had
4   recommended Carol to Buckner for an engagement somewhere out of town. It was dur-
5   ing that engagement that Buckner made his move on Carol. For a smart accountant,
6   Carol was young and not very worldly (she had married her high school sweetheart after
7   graduating from college), so she never really had a chance with the likes of Buckner.
8
9   Buckner's antics were well known in the firm. As Charles Milton's staff assistant, I took
10 notes for him during meetings of the firm's executive committee, of which he was a
11 member. Those notes were for his personal use; I don't have any idea if they still exist.
12 Charles was a stickler for throwing out paper after it was of no further use, so my guess
13 is those notes were destroyed years ago.
14
15 I specifically recall that when Charles was finishing his term as chair of the audit section
16 of the firm (he served from YR-10 until YR-5), the topic of Buckner as Charles's successor
17 was talked about, both around the firm and specifically in the firm's executive committee
18 meeting. Buckner wanted the position of the chair of the section, and the committee felt
19 hard pressed not to give it to him.
20
21 Despite his obvious failings and lack of morality, Buckner was regarded as the top part-
22 ner at attracting new clients to the firm. I know Charles often took Buckner along when
23 dealing with current clients and trying to attract new clients. Charles often referred to
24 Buckner as the next great "rainmaker" (one who attracts business to the firm) for C&S.
25 At the meetings leading up to Buckner's selection as chair, this was discussed openly in
26 both the executive committee and in the firm's rumor mill. The executive committee also
27 discussed, as did others informally, that the only drawbacks to Buckner as the chair was
28 that it might take away from his practice time, and whether it was wise to make Buckner
29 the chair, who would have the responsibility of evaluating all the young accountants in
30 the firm, including the women. I remember Charles saying in the executive committee
31 that having Buckner evaluating women accountants was like "having the fox guard the
32 henhouse."
33
34 In the end, the committee gave Buckner his wish and he was named chair of the audit
35 section. Bill Weisman, a very talented young partner with a good head on his shoulders
36 who was Buckner's protégé, was appointed as Buckner's deputy chair. The hope in the
37 committee was that Weisman could both lessen Buckner's administrative load, thereby
38 keeping him available for practice and client cultivation, and dissuade Buckner from go-
39 ing after the young women accountants.
40
41 After my conversation with Greg, I checked with a couple of my friends at C&S to see if
42 Professor Ahmed was suing the firm, and they confirmed she was. I was told she was su-
43 ing both Buckner and the firm for not being made partner. She claimed Buckner had ha-
44 rassed her and the firm knew about it and did nothing to stop him. That was consistent,

1 of course, with what I knew of Buckner and the way the rest of the firm treated him like
2 he could do no wrong.
3
4 I did not know of the lawsuit until I talked to Greg and checked it out with my old friends
5 at C&S. As I said, I work at Anderson & Jones now. I left C&S in YR-4 when Charles Milton
6 died right after his sixty-eighth birthday. Charles's death was shocking to me and my
7 family; it was the main reason my parents decided to retire shortly thereafter. The firm
8 informed me right after Charles's death that they would try to place me within the firm or
9 help me get a job outside the firm. I opted for the latter and got my position at Anderson
10 & Jones after Bill Weisman recommended me. I have no feelings, positive or negative,
11 towards the firm now Charles is no longer there.
12
13 Bill Weisman, who helped me get my current job, has also left the firm and taken an
14 executive position at Nita Computer World, one of C&S's best clients. The word from my
15 friends at C&S was that Bill left over the firm's treatment of Professor Ahmed. Shortly
16 after finding this out, I contacted Bill, and he confirmed what I had heard about Professor
17 Ahmed's lawsuit. He said he had agreed to act as a witness for Ms. Ahmed. I told Bill what
18 I have just told you and he put me in touch with you. I have voluntarily given this state-
19 ment to you, and I am available to testify at a deposition or trial, if necessary.

Materials for the Defendants

DEPOSITION OF PAUL BUCKNER

1 My name is Paul Buckner. I am fifty-two years old and married. My wife Amanda and
2 I have four children: Marla, who is twenty-eight; Paul Jr., who is twenty-four; Nora, who is
3 twenty-three; and Spencer, who is nineteen. Marla has a son, Grant, who is my only grand-
4 child. I am a partner in the accounting firm of Cooper & Stewart (C&S) here in Nita City.
5 I have recently stepped down as the chair of the audit section, after a three-year term. I am
6 considered one of the top attractors of new business (rainmakers) at the firm, and have a
7 national audit and audit litigation support practice. I am a member of the Nita State Soci-
8 ety of Certified Public Accountants (NSSCPA) and the American Institute of Certified Public
9 Accountants (AICPA). I am also on the Board of Directors of the Nita Chapter of the ACLU.
10
11 I am a YR-29 graduate of Yale University and a YR-27 graduate of the Yale Business School.
12 During those programs, I accumulated enough academic credits to qualify to sit for the
13 CPA exam, which I took and passed the summer after graduating from the business
14 school. After finishing my MBA program, I worked for three years in the civil division of
15 the U.S. Department of Justice in Washington, DC on cases that involved serious account-
16 ing issues. After one year of that practice (which satisfied the apprentice requirement) I
17 became a certified CPA. I joined C&S in YR-24 with a lateral transfer as a fourth-year ac-
18 countant. After the minimum three years at C&S, I was made a partner in the audit sec-
19 tion, where I have been ever since. I have always practiced in the audit section. Auditing
20 is the most challenging part of the accounting practice, in my view.
21
22 C&S has about sixty accountants. The number goes up and down a little each year as we
23 make partnership decisions at the top and hire new people at the bottom. Our only of-
24 fice is in Nita City. Our practice is concentrated in the four-state area, although there are
25 some members of the firm, who, like myself, have a clientele that is national in scope. We
26 are one of the largest firms in the city and like to think of ourselves as the best. There are
27 three sections in the firm: audit, tax, and small business.
28
29 The audit section is the largest with approximately thirty-five accountants, a third of
30 whom are partners and one of the partners is a woman. Audit has two women with ex-
31 cellent qualifications eligible for partner this year. The tax section has about fifteen or so
32 accountants. Tax has two women partners (Cheryl Stein and Kathryn Kowalski). The small
33 business section has ten or so accountants. It is designed to locate and provide services
34 to up-and-coming businesses, some of which succeed and become long-time, full-service
35 clients of the firm. We've also folded into this group the accountants who provide ser-
36 vices to clients who do not maintain any accounting staff. Danielle Reddick heads up the
37 small business group, and she has three other partners. Two of these are women part-
38 ners (Sherry Barker and Ann Feinman). You need partners there because the accounting
39 rules require partners in the firm to sign off on many of the forms and documents. In the
40 past, the small business group was not regarded as a quality practice like audit or tax, but
41 in my opinion, Danielle succeeded in building her practice, and they are well respected
42 within the firm.

1   I was the chief of the audit section of the firm, responsible for administering the evalu-
2   ation and partnership decisions in the firm. Yes, I can describe the process we utilize to
3   evaluate accountants. Each accountant is evaluated yearly on his anniversary date. The
4   chief and deputy chief of the section identify the partners for whom the accountant has
5   worked in the previous year and interview those partners to get their evaluations of
6   the accountant's performance. We also solicit the partners generally for additional com-
7   ments. We seek comments in the areas of analytical performance, writing skills, client
8   relations, attraction of new business, billable hours (with a 2200-hour benchmark), and
9   "collectable" billable hours (our benchmark is 80 percent collectable). Those evaluations
10   are compiled for each accountant into a summary and the accountant is assigned an eval-
11   uation of 1 to 5. Exhibits 3A–3G are the evaluation summaries for Ms. Ahmed; Exhibits
12   5A–5G are the evaluation summaries for Michael DeAngelo, who joined the firm at the
13   same level in the practice as Ms. Ahmed. I prepared several of those memos when I was
14   the chair of the audit section. The compilation of comments and evaluations are given
15   to all partners in the section for comments. The chief and the deputy then meet with
16   the accountant and communicate the evaluation and the underlying basis for the evalu-
17   ation. We do not divulge the source of comments, although sometimes the comment or
18   the context of the comment will indicate who made it. We also tell the accountant how
19   many people at approximately his level in the practice (ten to fifteen people) received
20   either the same or higher evaluation. The accountant receives a letter informing them of
21   their pay raise, which is tied directly to their assigned evaluation. The accountant does
22   not receive a copy of the evaluation memos, and they are destroyed when the accoun-
23   tant either leaves the firm or becomes a partner. The only records we maintain are the
24   evaluation each accountant receives and a copy of their pay letter. Exhibits 7A and 7B
25   are a compilation of the hours and evaluations for those accountants who were in Kiya
26   Ahmed's group.

28   The normal partnership track at C&S is six or seven years. Most people who make part-
29   ner have received an evaluation of 2 for at least two of their first four years, and 2's or
30   1's in their last three or four years before the partnership decision is made. It is unusual
31   for an accountant to make partner without at least one 1 evaluation, usually within a
32   year of the partnership decision. In addition to the evaluations earned, the accountant's
33   potential ability to attract business to the firm is an important factor in the partnership
34   decision.

36   The audit section nominates its accountants for partnership to the firm's executive com-
37   mittee, which then presents the candidates to the entire partnership for its consider-
38   ation. For an accountant to make partner, he must receive a majority vote of the entire
39   partnership. The nominations of the sections are usually followed except in extraordi-
40   nary circumstances.

42   Those accountants who do not meet our criteria leave the firm in a variety of ways. Some
43   accountants lack partnership potential because they do not interact well with clients but
44   have strong analytical skills. These accountants, who are usually identified in their third

1 or fourth year, may be offered a position as a senior accountant. These people are taken
2 off the partnership track; their compensation tops out at about the rate of a sixth-year
3 accountant.
4
5 Other accountants are given a certain time within which to find alternative employment.
6 Still others leave voluntarily to go to other firms, to government or teaching positions, or
7 because they leave the area for personal reasons. Finally, some accountants are identi-
8 fied as good potential employees for the financial offices of our clients. We will assist in
9 placing them with our clients, and usually they respond by continuing to send their busi-
10 ness to C&S.
11
12 That's an outline of the procedures we follow. If you need a more complete outline, the
13 best person I know to talk to is Bill Weisman. Bill was my deputy chief of audit and was
14 intimately involved in the evaluation process. He is currently the Vice President and Chief
15 Financial Officer of one of my best clients, Nita Computer World (NCW), and has been so
16 since April of YR-1. He was a partner in the firm for ten or eleven years before he left to
17 join NCW. Bill was one of my protégés at the firm. He is a very fine accountant who made
18 partner in only six years.
19
20 As I said, I have been with C&S for approximately twenty-four years. I chose this firm over
21 others for several reasons. First, my wife's family has lived in Nita City for five genera-
22 tions, and she wanted to live near her family. They own Preston Tools, Inc., a precision
23 tool manufacturing business. Preston Tools is one of C&S's clients—has been for at least
24 fifty years. Amanda's grandfather and Herb Cooper, one of C&S's founders, were the best
25 of friends. Since I'd narrowed my job search to the Nita City area, and partially because
26 of the family connection, I applied to C&S. I received offers from five of the six largest
27 firms in the city. C&S was willing to give me at least partial credit for my time in the Jus-
28 tice Department (in the end I was given full credit) towards a partnership decision while
29 the other firms were not. I accepted their offer, a decision I have never regretted. The
30 firm has grown nicely, and my personal audit practice is varied and interesting—over the
31 years it has become national in scope.
32
33 I am a very driven person. When I first started at C&S, some viewed me as having been
34 hired to satisfy a good client of the firm. I became obsessed with my accounting practice
35 and put in enormous hours at the firm. That hard work paid off professionally, and I am
36 now very well regarded. All that time and energy took its toll on my personal life though.
37 While I focused on my accounting practice, my wife focused on the children and her vari-
38 ous social and civic activities and, over the years, we have grown apart. To be honest, our
39 marriage is one of convenience. We have stayed together in name only and live separate
40 lives. The only time we spend any appreciable time together is over the holidays and on
41 family vacations. I'm sure if it wasn't for the children, we would have separated years
42 ago. But Amanda makes no demands on me other than whatever she gains socially from
43 being married to a successful accountant (she has inherited more money than I'll ever
44 have), so we have remained together, at least in name.

1　　I'll admit there have been times when I've considered asking her for a divorce, but each
2　　time I've done so Amanda threatened to poison my already tenuous relationships with
3　　my children, so I've always backed off. My children are very important to me, but my
4　　practice often requires me to be out of town, sometimes for several months at a time.
5　　This has prevented me from developing a normal father-child relationship with them.
6
7　　I am aware of my reputation at C&S of being an office Lothario. I suppose, to some ex-
8　　tent, it is deserved. Over the years I have had several sexual relationships with women at
9　　the firm, including both staff assistants and accountants, but nowhere near the number
10　　put out by the firm rumor mill. But I have never forced myself on anyone, nor used my
11　　position in the firm to obtain sexual favors. Each relationship has been freely entered into
12　　by both me and the woman involved. In fact, in many circumstances the woman was the
13　　aggressor in the relationship.
14
15　　These relationships normally evolve out of working long hours with the woman involved,
16　　under the stress of audit or expert witness testimony, especially in out-of-town litigation.
17　　Much of those engagements plays out in unfamiliar cities, and a natural sexual tension
18　　builds when two people work closely together on a common goal. As a result, the rela-
19　　tionships, because they are born out of a professional relationship involving a particular
20　　accounting engagement, often end when the engagement that brought the relationship
21　　about ends. When I am involved in these relationships, I am serious about them, and
22　　they are monogamous. Because the woman involved often feels guilty about an affair
23　　with a married man, there is often talk of my getting a divorce. To be honest, in some of
24　　these circumstances the relationship was, at the time, so satisfying that I truly believed
25　　it might lead to something permanent, which would require a divorce. In other circum-
26　　stances, I'll admit I talked of divorce to please my partner or ease her conscience, but
27　　actually had no intention of leaving Amanda.
28
29　　When these relationships have ended, their termination has often made the women in-
30　　volved uncomfortable in the firm. In some cases, their work performance slips and they
31　　have been let go. In other circumstances they have decided, given my leadership position
32　　in the firm, that they would be happier in another accounting position and have left for
33　　that reason. However, I have never forced a woman with whom I've had a relationship
34　　out of C&S. I have no reason to do so, and I wouldn't consider such a thing. I have never
35　　done anything that would hurt the professional opportunities at the firm of a woman
36　　with whom I have had a personal relationship. Specifically, I have never asked my part-
37　　ners to reduce their requests for the services of an accountant to lessen their billable
38　　hours, nor have I misrepresented the quality an accountant's work for me when I was
39　　asked for my evaluation as a part of our regular evaluation process. In fact, when women
40　　with whom I have had a personal relationship have left the firm, I have done everything
41　　I could to assist them in finding other suitable employment.
42
43　　It is true that most of the women with whom I have had a personal relationship are no
44　　longer with the firm, but that's true of most of the accountants we hire and most people

1 we hire as staff assistants. Of the maybe ten accountants we hire in every given year,
2 no more than three or four will become partners. Of those partners, approximately 25
3 percent leave the firm to go to other firms or to start their own firms. As for staff assis-
4 tants, most of our staff assistants only stay with the firm for four or five years at the most.
5 By that time, the good ones usually go graduate school or move out of the state and end
6 up employed with entities other than C&S, and the ones who are not so good are let go
7 by the firm for inadequate work performance.
8
9 There is one woman, with whom I had a brief personal relationship who is a current part-
10 ner at C&S. I prefer not to divulge her identity, because she was married at the time of
11 our relationship and is still married to the same person.
12
13 I have had approximately ten extramarital relationships with women who were or are
14 employees of C&S. To be honest, because many of them were for very short durations
15 and occurred many years ago I cannot remember all their names—the only such rela-
16 tionship that I have had in the past six years has been with Kiya Ahmed. If you suggest
17 the names of women with whom I am accused of having an affair, I will certainly confirm
18 or deny the fact, and tell you what I remember of the situation. I don't know anyone
19 who might recall their names except for Mary Langford, my longtime staff assistant, who
20 makes all my travel arrangements and handles my checking and credit card accounts.
21
22 I did have a relationship with a woman by the name of Susan McGinty, but that was easily
23 thirteen to fifteen years ago. She was a staff accountant with the firm. The only reason
24 I can time-frame the relationship is because it was during an engagement involving most
25 of the banks in Nita City and that lasted for approximately two years. That engagement
26 was the one in which I cemented my reputation with the firm as a quality expert witness.
27 Although I remember the engagement very well, I do not recall the relationship with
28 Ms. McGinty. I do know that she left the firm, but to be honest, I have no recollec-
29 tion of the circumstances. I recall her to be a competent accountant, but not someone
30 earmarked for partnership.
31
32 I do recall a relationship with a staff assistant by the name of Ellen Dorsen. That was
33 about ten to fifteen years ago. Ellen was a very aggressive young woman who worked
34 with me on an engagement in Memphis, Tennessee. The word on her among the male
35 accountants was she was only working at the firm in search of a husband. She was quite
36 young, I believe twenty-two or twenty-three. Ms. Dorsen initiated our relationship, com-
37 ing to my hotel room late one night on the first trip we made from Nita City to Memphis.
38 She was very attractive and given that I was substantially older than she—I was in my
39 forties, I think—I was flattered. Our relationship lasted the duration of that Memphis
40 engagement. The word got back to me that Ms. Dorsen was less than discrete about our
41 relationship, flaunting it quite openly, and that, together with the fact that I had tired of
42 her, caused me to break off our relationship. No, I never told Ms. Dorsen I would marry
43 her or leave my wife for her; our relationship was a purely sexual one. Ms. Dorsen left the
44 firm within a year of the ending of our relationship. I understand she was let go for poor

1   performance. I had no part in that decision, as those matters were handled by a commit-
2   tee that deals with staff assistants. I don't recall being contacted by the committee about
3   my evaluation of her work. If I was, I would have given my honest appraisal of her work,
4   which was that it was adequate.
5
6   I also recall a brief relationship with an accountant named Karen Newman. Our relation-
7   ship lasted about a month, which was the duration of an engagement on which she as-
8   sisted me in Dallas, Texas. Using the engagement as a marker, that would make it about
9   ten or eleven years ago. Ms. Newman was a bright young woman. I believe that she was
10 a midlevel staff accountant—third or fourth year—at the time. The relationship started
11 after we had spent many hours working closely together on the preparation for, and the
12 trial of that case. One thing sort of led to another and we ended up as lovers.
13
14 As I recall, Karen ended the relationship. She knew I was married and, although she was
15 bright and attractive, she knew I had no intention of leaving my wife for her, so she just
16 ended the affair. I don't know whether the subject of divorce ever came up with her;
17 I just don't remember. I'll admit she might have bruised my male ego, but I certainly did
18 not retaliate against her by damaging her career in any way. As I recall, Ms. Newman left
19 the firm about a year later and joined another firm in Nita City. I sent out, at her request,
20 a very good letter of recommendation, which I'm sure did not hurt her in obtaining an-
21 other position. I am generally regarded, both in the firm and in the community, as a good
22 judge of accounting talent. It is possible Bill Weisman might have drafted that letter for
23 me, but I just don't remember. He has done that sort of thing for me in the past.
24
25 And there was my relationship with Carol Merritt. At the time, I felt this relationship
26 would lead to a more permanent situation. Ms. Merritt was either a third- or fourth-
27 year staff accountant at the time of our relationship, which lasted for approximately nine
28 months. She was very well regarded in the firm: bright, articulate, and talented. As usual,
29 the affair began because we were involved together in an engagement. I was the partner
30 in charge of the engagement, and Carol was assigned to assist me.
31
32 The engagement was in Washington State and involved a situation in which an environ-
33 mental group publicly accused the client of misinforming the government. The crux of
34 the accusation involved complicated accounting papers and data the client filed with the
35 government about tree cutting in forests the client owned. Using the engagement as a
36 time post, that must have been about ten years ago. My relationship with Ms. Merritt
37 began while we were wading through the paperwork of that engagement and lasted
38 through the two-and-a-half-month trial of the case and beyond.
39
40 Ms. Merritt was married at the time to her childhood sweetheart; over time they had
41 apparently grown apart. Our relationship did not end, as was the usual pattern, with the
42 engagement. We were quite serious, and I truly believed at the time that I would divorce
43 my wife and marry Carol. I'm sure she and I talked about my getting a divorce, because
44 that was truly my intention. She, too, was quite serious. She left her husband and rented

1   an apartment, which I helped to finance. Our relationship lasted for about five months
2   after the engagement ended. I raised the issue of divorce with my wife on several occa-
3   sions, but she threatened to alienate my children from me. I backed down and ended the
4   relationship with Ms. Merritt. Amanda also threatened to sour my business relationship
5   with several of my clients who were also social friends of hers and her family, but it was
6   the threat to my relationships with my children that caused me to back off my request for
7   a divorce. The ending of the relationship devastated Carol. She took vacation and leave
8   from the firm for about a month, then came back in only to pack up her desk and resign.
9   She and her husband got their relationship back together and moved to Washington, DC.
10 I sent out letters of recommendation on her behalf, and she was hired by a very good firm
11 there. Bill Weisman might have drafted the letters; I just don't recall. I was the real loser
12 in that situation. Our relationship was a good one, much better than my relationship with
13 my wife.
14
15 After my relationship with Carol Merritt, I avoided another serious relationship within
16 the firm until Kiya Ahmed. There were several brief dalliances with staff assistants over
17 the next three years, but none of them were serious, and none lasted more than a couple
18 of weeks. All those women have left the firm for various reasons. I never forced anyone
19 out of the firm.
20
21 I did not have a relationship with an accountant during that time, perhaps because of the
22 difficulty with Ms. Merritt. My personal relationships never interfered with my profes-
23 sional judgment of an accountant or a staff assistant and I never forced anyone out of the
24 firm because of a failed personal relationship with me. As I said, there is a current partner
25 of the firm with whom I had a very brief romantic relationship. She was and is married
26 and I will not divulge her name unless the court orders it. The other women with whom
27 I've had relationships left before reaching the partnership decision stage, usually at their
28 own choosing. If any had come before the partners, I would do what I always do: give an
29 honest appraisal of the woman's accounting ability.
30
31 In YR-7, my son Spencer, who was then twelve years old, was involved in a serious ac-
32 cident while he was riding his bicycle. He was severely injured and for a time we weren't
33 sure whether he was going to make it, although eventually he made a full recovery. That
34 experience brought Amanda and me together and revived our marriage. We remained
35 close for several years, but eventually grew apart again. During that time, I had no extra-
36 marital affairs except for the brief flings I mentioned earlier. We were already emotion-
37 ally estranged when I got involved with Kiya Ahmed in YR-3.
38
39 Kiya started working for C&S over fifteen years ago. The first real contact I had with her
40 was when she worked with me as a staff assistant on the bank audit engagement in YR-
41 15 through YR-13. As I said, this was an important and complicated engagement, and
42 her work was exemplary. I was very impressed with her work, as was Bill Weisman, who
43 worked closely with me on that engagement. At the end of the engagement, I compli-
44 mented Ms. Ahmed on her work and suggested she go to graduate school to get an MBA

1   degree. Although I recommended she go full time, she was a single mother and needed to
2   work while in school. As a result, she went to Nita University in the online MBA program.
3
4   Ms. Ahmed continued to work at the firm time during her MBA program, and from time
5   to time she did work for me. Because she had a good deal of natural talent, and because
6   I liked her personally, I kept tabs on her school career. She did very well in graduate
7   school, while performing top-notch work as a staff assistant at the firm. I might have
8   discussed her progress with her from time to time, and now that you ask, I believe I took
9   her out to lunch once or twice to celebrate her successes at school. I had no interest in
10 her, other than professional, at that time. I might have occasionally commented that she
11 looked attractive or flirted with her. That is just the way I am. I am also a very physical
12 person. It is not uncommon for me to touch the person with whom I'm speaking, both
13 male and female. I might have done this with Kiya Ahmed, but I certainly didn't mean
14 anything by it, and I have no recollection of doing so. As I said, I had no personal interest
15 in her at that time.
16
17 I did go to bat for her during her first year as an accounting intern. Accounting interns do
18 not receive bonuses at C&S. That is because they are uniformly students who will only
19 be with the firm for a year—C&S does not permanently hire accounting interns and does
20 not have any long-term interest in them. I guess in the back of my mind I saw her as a
21 potential accountant. I argued with the then-chief of the audit section that she should
22 remain eligible for bonuses. He went along, and I gave her a bonus check for whatever
23 the first year of her working as a staff assistant would have been. I remember she was
24 quite excited to receive it, and very grateful.
25
26 As I said, Ms. Ahmed did some work for me during the three years in her MBA program,
27 all of it very high quality. I would have asked for her on more of my engagements but,
28 because of her situation as a single parent, she did not travel for extended periods of
29 time and most of my engagements were out of town. At any rate, her work was always
30 first-rate, and Bill Weisman—for whom she apparently did quite a bit of work—said her
31 work as an accounting intern was better than some of our accountants.
32
33 In YR-10, I was the chair of the hiring committee for the firm, and Bill Weisman was one
34 of its most active members. Bill approached me in the fall of YR-10 about hiring Kiya
35 Ahmed as a staff accountant in the firm. I pointed out to him that such a move was un-
36 precedented; up until that point, we had never hired an accounting intern as an accoun-
37 tant. We also had never hired a graduate of any online program as an accountant. Bill
38 argued that Kiya's work was first-rate, that there was no difference between Nita Univer-
39 sity's online education and the regular in-class program, and finally, that our applicants
40 for accountant positions for YR-10 had not been a particularly impressive group. I had to
41 agree with Bill that we were less impressed than normal with the group.
42
43 I agreed to quietly sound out the hiring committee on the prospect of hiring Kiya Ahmed.
44 Although there were some opposed, most agreed that she could be interviewed. Bill and

1   I approached Kiya and encouraged her to apply. We made it clear that it was not certain
2   she would receive an offer, but she would get a fair look and both of us would support
3   her. She seemed quite flattered and excited at the prospect. She applied that fall and
4   went through the interviewing process. There was some opposition, primarily because
5   she was an online program MBA student. The only other negative was her need to be
6   assigned to engagements that kept her predominantly in Nita City due to her responsi-
7   bilities as a single mother. As I've said, our practice has always covered a four-state area
8   and my own expert witness engagements have been national in scope. If I am an expert
9   witness, our accountants are often required to set up shop in the city where the case is
10 being litigated. Kiya's inability to do so presented the most substantive roadblock to her
11 receiving an offer. The most vociferous opponent to her hiring was Danielle Reddick who
12 is the partner in charge of the small business section of the firm. In the end we felt the
13 positives outweighed any negative and an offer was authorized. I conveyed our offer to
14 Kiya, and she accepted immediately. She seemed quite pleased and excited to start her
15 accounting career at C&S.
16
17 For Ms. Ahmed's first five years at the firm as a staff accountant, she did very little work
18 for me. That was predominantly because most of my practice requires the accountants
19 assigned to my engagements to travel out of town. What work she did do for me was
20 first-rate and justified our offer to her. She did a great deal of work for Bill Weisman, and
21 he was most complimentary of her abilities. I believe she was evaluated at the 3 level
22 for her first year, which is a typical evaluation. She received 2's in her second, third, and
23 fourth years. These evaluations are quite good and as of her fourth year she was consid-
24 ered a very good candidate for a partnership. There were some lingering questions about
25 her online graduate school work and her inability to travel, but she was doing quite well.
26 There were also some questions about her toughness and aggressiveness.
27
28 Yes, in her fourth year we received an email message from one of my older partners
29 in audits who commented that our clients would be unhappy if a firm representative
30 showed up at their business looking like a terrorist and soon we would have people wear-
31 ing burkas in the office. Bill replied for me that the partner's comments were inappropri-
32 ate and contrary to firm policy and that he should cease such comments immediately.
33 He was also informed that we had at least two practicing Muslims who were his partners
34 and numbers of other employees with mid-Eastern ethnicity and of the Muslim faith. Yes,
35 the emails you have shown me from YR-5 are the ones in question, and my lawyer says
36 they should have been withheld as privileged.
37
38 YR-4, Ms. Ahmed's fifth with the firm, was a horrible one for her. There were some seri-
39 ous negative comments about the quality of her work and her billable hours were down
40 substantially. Those two factors often go hand in hand. If there are problems with an
41 accountant's work, fewer partners will request that accountant to work on their engage-
42 ments. As a result, billable hours decrease. Bill Weisman told me that Kiya lost her father
43 after a two-month illness, which required her out to be of town frequently. In addition,
44 her teenage children had also had rough years, as teenagers often do. Bill said these

1 events coincided and explained Kiya's poor performance. By that time, I was chief of the
2 audit section, so I heard the complaints about Kiya's work personally, as did Bill Weisman,
3 whom I had selected to be my deputy.
4
5 In Ms. Ahmed's fifth year, I did the best I could with her evaluation, but the highest evalu-
6 ation we could justify was a 3. An evaluation of 3 in the fifth year of an accountant's
7 career usually spells the end of his association with the firm. Sometimes we will assist
8 the accountant in finding a job with a client, but usually the accountant is given a good
9 recommendation and finds a new position on their own. In Ms. Ahmed's case, at my in-
10 sistence, my partners approved a third alternative for her. I was about to enter into a fast-
11 tracked audit on behalf of Nita Computer World. They were alleged to have participated
12 in a price fixing scheme with other retailers of computer hardware and software, and
13 I needed a senior accountant on the engagement. My partners agreed that if I was willing
14 to take the risk, they would as well.
15
16 Bill and I presented the evaluation to Kiya and gave her the alternatives I just mentioned.
17 As we expected, she chose to sign onto the NCW engagement, even though I made it
18 clear that there was some substantial travel involved in the engagement. Her children were
19 older by then, and she said they had gotten through their rough patch. Her son was a junior
20 or senior in high school, so she felt that she could leave them for a few days at a time.
21
22 Our faith in Kiya was well placed, given her performance on the NCW case. She did a
23 superb job and her work was recognized not just by me, but by the two other partners on
24 the engagement. In fact, her research for an important protective order against discovery
25 of some NCW trade secrets was so successful that NCW's General Counsel sent a letter
26 complimenting her specifically. (See Exhibit 6.)
27
28 During the NCW engagement, which ran nonstop from late September of YR-4 through
29 June of YR-3, Kiya and I were in constant contact. She often traveled with me or one of
30 the other partners when motions were argued or for depositions. Kiya was present for all
31 the strategy and case theory sessions. As the case heated up, depositions were scheduled
32 in clusters and Kiya participated in many of the prep sessions, which usually were held
33 in my suite. When the work for the day was over, we often ordered a late meal or some
34 wine to unwind and relax. This occurred with other members of the litigation team pres-
35 ent, although sometimes we were alone. Over the course of the audit we became closer,
36 talking often about personal matters. She told me all about her marriage and family, and
37 I did the same. There was no sexual relationship, although I'll admit I was attracted to
38 her, but we did develop a close personal relationship. She sent some signals that she was
39 interested in a physical relationship—by the way she looked at me, or by the touch of her
40 hand—but although my wife and I were back to our separate lives, nothing came of it. I
41 do not recall making any sexual advances towards her during the time of the audit.
42
43 The case settled on extremely favorable terms to NCW in June of YR-3. NCW thanked the
44 litigation team by sending us on a week's vacation to the Bahamas. Spouses were invited,

1 but neither Kiya nor I brought anyone along. It was during this vacation that we became
2 physically intimate. I don't think either one of us intended it to happen, it just seemed
3 like the natural progression in our relationship.
4
5 The beginning of my relationship with Kiya Ahmed was different than others I had with
6 women at the firm. In all the other relationships, the physical relationship was first, fol-
7 lowed in some cases, such as with Carol Merritt, by a more meaningful relationship. With
8 Kiya Ahmed, the relationship just evolved naturally.
9
10 I was convinced Kiya and I would eventually marry, and we started to make plans for our
11 lives together. We spent a great deal of time together and everything seemed to be work-
12 ing out well. I told her I wanted to wait to file for divorce until my son Spencer was enrolled
13 in college and away from home. When he had a hard time adjusting to college, I put off the
14 divorce until the end of the first semester. Kiya was very understanding about my concern
15 for Spencer initially, but grew increasingly impatient. She became very upset when I went
16 to a family gathering on Labor Day of YR-3, where I saw my first grandchild for the first time,
17 and when I insisted on spending what I thought would be my last family gathering over the
18 holidays in December of YR-3 and January of YR-2. I planned to tell Amanda that I was filing
19 for divorce after that holiday, but Spencer was still not doing very well in his transition to
20 college. I determined that in his interest, I should wait until the end of the first year.
21
22 In the end, Kiya just could not be patient. She gave me an ultimatum in January of YR-2:
23 file for divorce or end our relationship. Because of my son, I just couldn't do it, so I lost
24 her. Kiya made the decision to part, not me. Fortunately, I had an engagement that took
25 me away for several months and the work let me heal my wounds. I was hurt when the
26 relationship ended, but I never made any threats to her professional career at C&S and
27 never did anything that was intended to harm her and her position at the firm. I do not
28 recall the specifics of my conversation with Kiya on the day she ended our relationship.
29 I certainly never threatened her personally, nor her employment at the firm. I do re-
30 member offering to take her on a trip, but she turned me down. In March of YR-2, when
31 I returned from my engagement, I called and asked Kiya out to dinner, but she declined.
32
33 I understand Kiya had some difficulty as well—she had some health problems that caused
34 her to be out of the office, and, in addition, the quality of her work slipped. No one wants
35 to assign work to an accountant, especially a senior accountant, whose work product is
36 unreliable, so I'm not surprised her billable hours decreased. This was a shame; based on
37 her work on the NCW engagement, Kiya had been evaluated at the 1 level for her sixth
38 year and seemed on track to be made partner in June of YR-2—particularly since, after
39 the NCW engagement, she continued to perform at a very high level until the winter and
40 spring of YR-2. Through that time, we had every indication that Kiya's difficulty in YR-5
41 had been a one-time problem.
42
43 I certainly had nothing to do with the drop-off in Kiya's work. That was a result of her per-
44 formance, and to suggest I had anything to do with it is ridiculous. If anything, because

1   I was so effusive (and rightfully so on the merits) about Kiya's performance on the NCW
2   engagement, she received more than her share of quality assignments in YR-3. That they
3   did not continue is her own doing.

4

5   The drop-off in work was certainly apparent from the comments Bill Weisman received
6   while preparing Kiya's evaluation for the meeting on partnership by the audit section in
7   June of YR-2. Because of my relationship with Kiya, I thought it best that Bill take charge
8   of the evaluation. After reviewing those comments and consulting with me, he suggested
9   to Kiya that she put off her partnership decision until YR-1 so that she could repair her
10   reputation, which had been damaged by her poor (for her) quality work. In the end she
11   did not take our advice. Even though I spoke in her favor, she was not nominated for part-
12   nership. Because our relationship was common knowledge within the firm, I abstained
13   in the vote, but that abstention had no effect on the outcome, because, as chair, I only
14   voted in the case of a tie, and there was not a tie vote on her candidacy. Bill said she
15   asked to be reconsidered in a year, but the partnership decision was final. The issue of
16   offering Ms. Ahmed a senior accountant position was never raised—the question of her
17   reliability and performance under pressure meant she was not a good candidate for a
18   permanent non-partner position.
19

20   At the meeting, the primary concern was Kiya's response to personal difficulties. Our
21   clients expect high quality accounting work from us, no matter what else is happening
22   in our lives. Kiya, within three years, had shown two times when she wasn't able to put
23   aside personal problems and remain focused on her work. In the end, that is what, in my
24   opinion, killed her candidacy.

25

26   As is typical in these situations, we gave Kiya a six-month grace period to find another
27   position. I always thought she would go on and be successful in the accounting field,
28   although I understand she had a hard time finding another position with an account-
29   ing firm. I did write and send out several recommendation letters on her behalf when
30   requested to do so by potential employers. (See Exhibits 11, 12, 13.) I did not send out
31   the letter drafted for me by Bill Weisman. (See Exhibit 10.) I thought the letter was too
32   effusive and not an accurate reflection of my opinion of Kiya's abilities, so I drafted my
33   own letter. Yes, by the time I drafted that letter I knew Kiya had complained to the EEOC.
34   It might have occurred to me that an overly effusive letter could later be used against us
35   in some legal proceeding, but the letter I drafted was based on my honest assessment of
36   Kiya's abilities.

37

38   I have looked at Exhibit 11 and can identify the first handwritten note on the bottom of
39   the letter as my own. The second notation is not in my handwriting. John Randall is an
40   old and close friend. His forensic accounting practice focuses predominantly on white-
41   collar-criminal defense. C&S has always provided accounting services in what you'd call
42   civil matters, but my expert testimony tends to involve the same kinds of transactions
43   that sometimes find their way into criminal court. For that reason, I thought Kiya's resume
44   might be attractive to him. On the other hand, his practice is much more pressurized and

1 fast-paced than ours; given Kiya's history at the firm of having trouble separating per-
2 sonal crises from professional performance, I did not think she was a good fit. I don't
3 recall if I spoke to John Randall on the phone, but if I did, I'm sure I said to him what
4 I just said to you about Kiya's fit with that firm. Looking at Exhibits 8 and 9, I can identify
5 them as my phone logs for the dates shown. The check marks are mine. They mean that
6 I returned the calls checked off. They do not mean that I ever actually spoke to the people
7 I called back. I do not recall speaking to anyone else about Kiya Ahmed by way of giving
8 her a reference. I might have; I just don't recall.
9
10 Not using Bill's draft of a recommendation letter for Kiya caused me some problems with
11 Bill. He came in to talk to me about it sometime in early YR-1. Apparently, he told Kiya
12 I would send out the letter he had drafted. I told him what I told you about why I had
13 written my own letter. It was my attempt to give an honest appraisal of Kiya's abilities and
14 not in any way an attempt to do her any harm.
15
16 Kiya decided on a teaching career and is now on the faculty at the University of Nita
17 School of Law as a practice professor teaching accounting related courses to law stu-
18 dents. I understand she is doing very well, and I wish her well. I sent a letter on her behalf
19 to the dean of the law school, Marty Purcell, who was an undergraduate classmate of
20 mine at Yale. The letter may have been a form of the letter Bill Weisman drafted for me.
21 It is different from the letter I sent to the accounting firms back in YR-2, mainly because
22 the job requirements are different. I truly believe Kiya will flourish in the more sheltered
23 environment of academia.
24
25 The others at Kiya's level who came up for partnership in YR-2, Mark Hancock and Roger
26 Kramer, were easy choices. Mark had distinguished himself during an important engage-
27 ment in the spring of YR-2 and the client made it clear that Mark should be assigned to
28 their future engagements. Roger had been a very solid performer and was also the son
29 of the president of one of our best clients. Mike DeAngelo was put off for a year to see
30 if he could improve his performance in the area of client relations. He ended up having
31 a good year, attracted a new client to the firm, and was granted partnership in June of
32 YR-1. Although it might appear that Mike and Kiya were treated differently, in that Mike
33 was allowed another year to improve, the engagements are really different. Mike had
34 been a rock-solid, consistent performer and we were just looking for a little spark to push
35 him over the edge. Kiya had shown brilliance and real lows, and another year would not
36 dispel the concern that her work would suffer every time she encountered a personal
37 problem.
38
39 I know Bill Weisman believes I am responsible for Kiya's not making partner. In reality,
40 however, I did nothing to hurt her chances; it was all her own doing. I never did or said
41 anything that was intended to harm her work assignments or the way she was regarded
42 in the firm. Most of what occurred that hurt her happened while I was out of town.
43 I know Bill is particularly angry with me, but he has always been overly involved in Kiya
44 Ahmed's promotion within the firm, and he is just disappointed. I assume he'll get over

1   it in time. We have maintained a good professional relationship since he has moved over
2   to NCW. He is my contact at NCW and has corporate responsibility for overseeing C&S's
3   performance on audit matters we handle for them.
4
5   In September of YR-2, I stepped down as the chief of the audit section. Although the
6   normal term in five years and I had not completed my term, I thought I was out of town
7   on engagements too frequently to properly administer the section, so Steve Ibanez took
8   over. To maintain continuity, Bill Weisman stayed on as his deputy until he left C&S in
9   YR-1. In no way was my relationship with Kiya Ahmed related to my leaving the position.
10
11   As I mentioned earlier, the EEOC notified us that Ms. Ahmed had filed a complaint against
12   us in the summer of YR-2. (See Exhibit 14.) I was consulted about our response, and, in
13   a letter written by our lawyer, the firm's chair, Rob Bryant, responded with a general de-
14   nial. (See Exhibit 15.) In December of YR-2 the EEOC notified us they had issued a "right
15   to sue" letter to her, so the filing of this lawsuit is not surprising. (See Exhibit 16.) It is,
16   however, in my opinion, unjustified. No decision at C&S regarding Ms. Ahmed was ever
17   motivated by a sexually discriminatory act. She just failed to make the evaluation, on the
18   merits. I'm sorry it turned out that way, but it did.

I have read this deposition and it is complete and accurate.

Paul Buckner

Paul Buckner

Subscribed and sworn before me this 12th day of July, YR-0.

Harry Gibbons

Harry Gibbons
Certified Shorthand Reporter

This deposition was taken in the office of the counsel for the defendants on July 1, YR-0. This deposition was given under oath and was read and signed by the deponent.

DEPOSITION OF DANIELLE REDDICK

1   My name is Danielle Reddick. I am forty-six years old and a partner in the accounting firm
2   of Cooper & Stewart (C&S). I am married to Harvey Wilkes, and we live at 25 Woodcrest
3   Place in Nita City. Harvey owns a small construction business in Nita City. We do not have
4   any children. Our careers didn't leave time to properly raise children, so we decided against
5   becoming parents.
6
7   I graduated from Yale University in YR-24 with a BA degree in English. I graduated with
8   honors from Yale, and three years later, in YR-21, I graduated with honors with a master's
9   degree in accounting and finance from the University of Toronto in Canada. That same year
10   I settled with my husband in Nita City, and I took and passed the Nita CPA exam. I got a job
11   as an accountant at Cooper & Stewart. At that time, I was one of two women profession-
12   als in the firm which had about thirty accountants, three or four of whom were partners.
13   There were no women partners in the audit section when I started with the firm. When
14   I was made a partner in the firm in YR-13, I was the first woman partner in audits.
15
16   Rather than remain in the audit section, I persuaded my partners to open a small business/
17   accounting services section of the firm. We take on smaller clients, build good relation-
18   ships, and hope that they succeed. When they do, they usually become full-service clients
19   of the firm. We have met some good success and our future appears bright.
20
21   The firm now has six women partners. Two partners, Sherry Barker and Ann Feinman, work
22   with me in my small business group. They became partners in YR-10 and YR-3 respectively.
23   Cheryl Stein and Kathryn Kowalski work in the tax group. They became partners in YR-6 and
24   YR-3 respectively. Currently, there is only one woman partner in the audit group, although
25   there are two strong candidates in the pipeline.
26
27   C&S does not have the longest history of treating women fairly in hiring and partnership
28   decisions, but I'd say in the thirteen years I have been a partner that women have received
29   equal opportunities in the firm. Since I have been a partner, I have made sure of that. This
30   is true for a variety of reasons. First, the main opposition to women accountants in the firm
31   came from some of the partners who were most senior when I joined the firm. These peo-
32   ple have since retired or have been silenced by the majority in the firm. Second, women are
33   now getting CPA licenses at about the same rate as men (unlike when I was in school), and if
34   the firm wants the most-talented professionals, it's necessary to hire women. At C&S, talent
35   is the most important quality for an accountant, so we have, for at least the last five years,
36   been hiring about the same number of men and women at the starting level in the firm.
37
38   Women are working their way through the firm to partnership and in YR-3, two women,
39   Georgia Bratton and Kathryn Kowlaski, were made partner, while only one man, Dave
40   Hamilton, made the evaluation. All partners in the firm are equity partners. We have con-
41   sidered granting non-equity partnerships in cases where the candidate is highly qualified

1   but lacks the ability to attract or keep clients. That has not yet occurred, although I am sure
2   it will in the future.

3

4   I'll admit when I was coming through the firm it was a struggle for a woman. Even though
5   the new hires in my group were almost 40 percent women, the senior partners were ini-
6   tially unwilling to give the more challenging and important assignments to the women
7   accountants. I had to fight to get good assignments in order to get recognized within the
8   firm and, even when I did a good job, it never seemed to be enough. During my evaluations
9   I constantly received comments that questioned my aggressiveness, although no one
10   could give any examples of my not being aggressive enough. It was a tough struggle, but
11   eventually I was recognized for my talent. One thing in my favor is that I worked mainly
12   in the audit section, which gave me the most visibility, although it still had a men's club
13   atmosphere as the more prestigious section. The other main thing in my favor, I think,
14   was my billable hours were always first or second at my level in the firm. I was also willing
15   to travel anywhere, at any time, and never turned down an assignment, no matter how
16   pushed I was. Fortunately for me, my husband was very understanding and he stuck with
17   me over the years. Although it took eight years, as opposed to the then-normal seven, to
18   make partner, I hung on and worked extremely hard and made the evaluation as the first
19   woman partner in audit.

20

21   There were two things in the final analysis that got me over the partnership hump. First,
22   I worked on an engagement with Paul Buckner in YR-16, and he was very complimentary
23   of my work to his partners. Paul was, at the time, a rising star in the firm (he was in his late
24   thirties then) and his comments to his partners helped me get good assignments where
25   I could show my abilities. I also know Paul persuaded his partners to give me an extra
26   year to make partner and spoke very highly of my abilities during the partnership meet-
27   ing at which I was nominated for partnership. And even though it seems counterintuitive,
28   the second thing was my willingness to work on and succeed in small business matters.
29   Although it started as a reflection of my apparent second-class citizenship in the firm,
30   I gained the respect of several of our best corporate clients by working for the start-up
31   companies formed by friends and relatives of the executives. That translated into respect
32   in the firm. I enjoyed the work and the independence it gave me within the firm. Because
33   the work was not mainline audit or tax work, most of the partners did not want to become
34   involved in it, so I had a great deal of autonomy and could showcase my abilities.

35

36   It was for that reason that once I made partner, even though I was entitled to work in the
37   audit section, I persuaded my partners to let me build a small business section within the
38   firm. Although initially reluctant, they finally agreed, and I now have a thriving practice.
39   There are now four partners in my group, including myself, and we have about ten or so
40   accountants working with us. Three of the partners are women. One of them is a man—
41   yes, he is Caucasian. This is more by happenstance than design. Because I made it a point
42   to give our women accountants plenty of work when they needed it, and I involved them
43   in the full range of business issues when some of my partners would not, some women
44   naturally gravitated to my group. In addition, I have actively promoted women within the

1   firm and served as a mentor for many of them. The accountants who now work in my
2   group are about evenly split between men and women, and I expect within a few years, as
3   long as our business keeps growing, one of the men will be made a partner in the firm and
4   continue to work in my group.
5
6   I think I have the respect of my partners, but I know some elitism concerning the various
7   sorts of practice within the firm remains. Some members of the firm view small business as
8   less demanding than the run-of-the-mill audit and tax work. For that reason, I have always
9   counseled the women accountants to seek out a well-rounded selection of assignments,
10 so they can showcase their talents. Even if they prefer to specialize in either small business
11 or accounting services, they need exposure to the other accountants and for all the part-
12 ners to be familiar with them and the quality of their work. This is the kind of advice young
13 accountants need to hear at C&S, and I have made sure over the years that the women
14 accountants have gotten the same good advice that the men, with their mentors, got when
15 I was coming up through the ranks. I can't recall specifically speaking to Ms. Ahmed about
16 that advice, but she was somewhat aloof when it came to me and I know Bill Weisman
17 looked after her and helped her find her way through the firm.
18
19 The firm evaluates staff accountants annually. The process requires the section chief and
20 deputy section chief to interview all the partners for whom the accountant has done work
21 during the year, solicit comments from the rest of the firm members, and review the ac-
22 countant's billable hours. With all this information, they form an evaluation ranging from
23 1 to 5. The evaluation, and the basis for the evaluation, is then reviewed with the accoun-
24 tant. If their evaluations do not meet the requirements for partnership, the accountants
25 know early so that they can either improve or choose to move on to another firm or an-
26 other position within the profession. The accountant also learns how many other accoun-
27 tants at their level in the firm got the same evaluation, and how many did better, so they
28 can rank themselves. Exhibits 3A–3G, and Exhibits 5A–5H, the evaluation memos concern-
29 ing Kiya Ahmed and Michael DeAngelo, are typical examples of the form, and reflect the
30 kind of information the firm provides to our accountants by way of evaluation.
31
32 During the staff accountant's first four years, the typical evaluation is 3, with people who
33 achieve 2's on a regular basis making up the top three or four people being evaluated. At the
34 fourth year, some accountants are told to seek other employment, some are assisted in find-
35 ing jobs with one of our clients (which promotes good relations with the former accountant
36 and the client) and some accountants, who are intellectually able but lacking in the people
37 skills necessary to make partner, are offered jobs as permanent senior accountants. These
38 people usually earn about the same salary as sixth-year accountants but have no possibility
39 of ever becoming a partner. The fifth and sixth years are important for those accountants who
40 will make partner; during those years they must show themselves to be special. The fifth- and
41 sixth-year accountant should be evaluated at level 1 if they expect to be made partner.
42
43 The partnership decision is normally made during June of the accountant's seventh year,
44 but can be put over to the eighth year. At that time, the partners vote on whether to

1 nominate the accountant for partnership. The accountant must receive a majority vote of
2 the partners in the section. In unusual circumstances the accountant may be given another
3 year to show his or her abilities, but usually if the vote is negative the accountant is given
4 six months in which to find another position. If the accountant is nominated for partner-
5 ship, his or her name is sent to the firm's Executive Committee, which then presents the
6 accountant to the entire partnership. I have never seen the Executive Committee fail to
7 present a section's nominee to the entire partnership. The nominee must receive a major-
8 ity vote from the entire partnership. The partnership considers the accountants' evalua-
9 tions, giving additional positive consideration to accountants who demonstrate the ability
10 to attract business to the firm.

12 As I said earlier, Paul Buckner was instrumental in getting his partners to give me a fair shot
13 at C&S, and for that I will be forever grateful. He evaluated me on my ability, not my gender,
14 when others were not willing to do so. He is, as I'm sure you know, the top business-getter
15 and expert witness at C&S. He is also very active in pro bono work for the Nita chapter of
16 the ACLU. His abilities are responsible for attracting and keeping many of the firm's major
17 clients. I respect him as an accountant, but he does have a fatal flaw.

19 Paul Buckner has, from what I have picked up over the years, a well-deserved reputation
20 as a womanizer. He is apparently married in name only and he and his wife must have an
21 understanding of some sort, because during my time with the firm he has had several
22 well-publicized affairs with either staff assistants or accountants in the firm—and there are
23 rumors of many more such affairs. No, I am not one of those women. Paul's proclivities are
24 the source of some embarrassment to the firm. His behavior has been tolerated over the
25 years, and it probably would not have been but for his extraordinary business-attraction
26 (rainmaking) ability.

28 Although I know none of the details, I am aware that during a period of three of four years
29 about ten to fifteen years ago he had several public relationships with firm employees.
30 The women I know of are a staff assistant by the name of Ellen Dorsen, and accountants
31 by the names of Karen Newman, Susan McGinty, and Carol Merritt. None of these women
32 are still with the firm. Of the four, I know Karen Newman is an accountant here in Nita
33 City. I have no information about any of the others. I don't know the circumstances under
34 which they left the firm, as I wasn't particularly close to any of those women. Given Paul's
35 position of prominence in the firm, even back then, and the fact that they were in lesser
36 positions, I can only assume that they figured out it would be more comfortable for them
37 to be somewhere else.

39 I don't believe they were forced to leave. The firm would never be involved in any activ-
40 ity of that sort. But in such a situation, if the firm had to choose at some point between
41 an extremely talented and productive partner and an unproven accountant, the business
42 decision would seem obvious to me. That's not discrimination; that's just business. For-
43 tunately, we have never had to make such a stark decision, although in the case of Kiya
44 Ahmed, some of my partners might have viewed the partnership decision in that manner.

1   If they did so, they were deciding on a purely business basis, but I think denying her part-
2   nership was an appropriate decision on the merits.
3
4   Ms. Ahmed started to work for C&S as a staff assistant. I don't know the precise date but
5   I believe it was over fifteen years ago. At some point she decided to complete the neces-
6   sary accounting course work she had begun in undergraduate school by getting an MBA
7   degree. She did so by attending the online program offered by the University of Nita. With
8   the necessary course works completed, she could take the CPA exam and get her license.
9   During the time she was in the MBA program, she became an accounting intern at the firm.
10
11   In YR-10, I was one of the members of the hiring committee chaired by Paul Buckner. An-
12   other partner on the committee was Bill Weisman. At that time, Bill was a new partner
13   in the firm, having received a partnership offer in his sixth year as an accountant, a year
14   before anyone else at his level. Bill was an extraordinarily bright graduate of the University
15   of Nita (our first partner from that school) and Paul Buckner's protégé.
16
17   Paul Buckner and Bill put Ms. Ahmed's name forward as a potential accountant. At that
18   point, no accounting intern from the firm had ever been made an offer to become an ac-
19   countant. This policy was a good one, I think, because it kept the interns focused on their
20   work, and not on advancing their careers by making political connections within the firm. In
21   addition, we had never made an offer to a graduate of any online program. Some partners
22   felt the online program was less rigorous than the regular program and, although by that
23   point we had our first partner (Bill) and several accountants who were graduates of Nita
24   University, we had never hired anyone from the online program. Personally, I had no infor-
25   mation about the difference, if any, between the online program and the regular in-class
26   program. I did feel the full-time study of accounting, free from the distractions of work, was
27   a better way to learn the field—but that's probably because that's the way I went to school.
28
29   Paul Buckner approached me personally about hiring Ms. Ahmed. I'll have to say that be-
30   cause it violated our unwritten policy, I was initially opposed. Paul persuaded me that there
31   was no harm in interviewing her. He said she had done some good work for him, and Bill
32   was particularly impressed with her. I reluctantly agreed to her going through the process.
33
34   Ms. Ahmed was very impressive in her interview. I also reviewed some of her analytical
35   work (she had never done any work for me) and it demonstrated excellent skills, even
36   though the writing style was a little wordy—a not uncommon ailment for most of our ac-
37   countants. Her grades were also excellent; she graduated magna cum laude and first in her
38   class. I also considered it a bonus to her candidacy that she was of Middle-Eastern ethnicity
39   and a practicing Muslim. We have a strict policy against discrimination based on ethnicity
40   or religion, and while I know of at least a few practicing Muslims among the partners, there
41   were no Middle Easterners, and not enough women of any sort.
42
43   In the end, despite Ms. Ahmed's qualifications, I was not positive on her appointment. The
44   turning point for me was that, although she was interested in working in audit, she was

1   adamant about avoiding engagements with travel outside of Nita City for extended periods
2   of time. This was because she was the single parent of two children.
3
4   While I was sympathetic to her request, I thought it was unfair to the other accountants,
5   as well as to the firm. The other accountants in the firm would have to bear the burden of
6   the out-of-town work that would normally be hers.
7
8   The firm would also be deprived of the ability to evaluate her performance under the
9   stress of working in unfamiliar work environments. C&S has a four-state practice. We take
10   engagements wherever our clients do business, and particularly in audit, this sometimes
11   takes out accountants even further than the four-state area. As a result, Ms. Ahmed's limi-
12   tations on travel made it impossible for the firm to get a complete reading on how she
13   would likely perform as a partner.
14
15   In the end, however, my arguments did not prevail. Bill Weisman, and to a lesser extent
16   Paul Buckner, were very positive about her appointment and their opinion carried the day.
17   They were probably successful, at least in part, because the YR-10 group of applicants was
18   not very strong for some reason. Ms. Ahmed's application was probably viewed more fa-
19   vorably than it would have been in a more normal year.
20
21   Ms. Ahmed's first four years at the firm went very well. She was evaluated at the 2 level
22   for at least three of those years and appeared to be doing a good job. She did very little
23   work for me, but when she did, it was good. She was by far not the best accountant to
24   work for me, but her work was acceptable, and she responded well to comments I made
25   on her work for me. Bill Weisman took upon himself the role of her mentor; he guided her
26   to some of the larger engagements for our bigger clients, which, according to the conven-
27   tional wisdom at C&S, was the best way for an accountant to get a good reputation within
28   the firm. Advice that I agree with.
29
30   I continued, during that time, to question whether it was appropriate for an accountant
31   to get a free ride on the demanding out-of-town practice that was required of our ac-
32   countants, but to no avail. It seemed to me that Ms. Ahmed's children, who were then
33   teenagers, were old enough to be left for extended periods of time with hired childcare
34   professionals. After all, accountants were normally not out of town more than four nights a
35   week; usually they flew home on Friday evenings and back out on Monday mornings. This
36   was the routine when I was a staff accountant and remains the routine today. At any rate,
37   given her evaluations, my qualms aside, and with the active support and guidance of Bill
38   Weisman, Ms. Ahmed seemed to be on track to a partnership. I now know about a random
39   email to Paul and Bill regarding Ms. Ahmed's ethnicity and religion from an older partner,
40   since retired, in her fourth year in YR-5, that was rebuffed by Paul and Bill, and those facts
41   were never considered in employment related decisions regarding Ms. Ahmed.
42
43   Ms. Ahmed's performance changed in her fifth year, which ended in YR-4. For personal
44   reasons that I've never been clear on, except to the extent that I think it involved the

1   death of a parent or some problems with her children, Ms. Ahmed's work fell off dramati-
2   cally. There were real questions expressed about the quality of her work, and her billable
3   hours were down significantly. She was ultimately evaluated at the 3 level, which normally
4   would call for the firm giving her a certain time in which to find alternative employment.
5   And that's what would have happened but for the intervention of Paul Buckner, who by
6   that time was chief of the audit section. Paul persuaded the partners in the section to
7   allow him to present several alternatives to Ms. Ahmed. First, she could seek other em-
8   ployment. Second, Paul could recommend her for a job with the finance office of Nita
9   Computer World (NCW); they are a good client of his and would undoubtedly have hired
10 her on his recommendation. Finally, she could work with Paul and his team on a very com-
11 plicated and fast-tracked engagement for NCW to see if she could make up for her bad
12 year. Although there was some opposition in the section, the partners went along with
13 Paul's recommendation and the alternatives were presented to Ms. Ahmed. She opted for
14 working on the NCW engagement.
15
16 Her decision was a good one for her because, according to Paul and the other partners
17 who worked on the engagement, her work on the case was exemplary. I have also seen a
18 letter from NCW that singles her out for praise on the work she did. (See Exhibit 6.) Based
19 in part on that performance, she received very good assignments from other partners and
20 continued to work at a high level. As a result, Ms. Ahmed was evaluated at level 1 for her
21 sixth year and seemed to be positioned to make partner in June of YR-2.
22
23 Unfortunately for Ms. Ahmed, she also began a personal relationship with Paul Buckner.
24 The rumors about Paul had subsided during the several years before the NCW case, so
25 I was surprised when I heard about the relationship. There was no doubt, however, that
26 she was involved with Paul and the rumors were Paul was going to divorce his wife and
27 marry Ms. Ahmed.
28
29 The personal relationship between Ms. Ahmed and Paul Buckner made me wonder about
30 the validity of her performance evaluation. That is, I was concerned Paul was not evaluat-
31 ing her solely on job performance and that other partners were giving good references to
32 please Paul as opposed to on the merits. I therefore requested Ms. Ahmed be assigned to a
33 complicated distribution of assets case I had involving the division of several corporations.
34 I thought this case would demonstrate Ms. Ahmed's abilities, and therefore I could be
35 comfortable in voting for her partnership. My request for her assistance was turned down,
36 however, because she was working with Bill Weisman on another matter for NCW at the
37 same I time I needed her, so she never worked for me.
38
39 In January of YR-2, the relationship between Paul Buckner and Ms. Ahmed apparently
40 ended. For that or other personal reasons, Ms. Ahmed's work leading up to the partner-
41 ship decision date in June of YR-2 again dropped off in terms of quality and quantity. I know
42 Bill Weisman counseled Ms. Ahmed to put off going forward for partner for a year, but she
43 refused to do so. As a result, we had a rather rancorous meeting considering whether she
44 should become a partner.

1   In the end, the partners' concern about Ms. Ahmed's inability to separate her personal life
2   from her professional life caused her not to be made a partner. The argument that pre-
3   vailed was that in two of the three years leading up to the partnership decision, a personal
4   problem had caused Ms. Ahmed's work to drop off. That behavior cannot be tolerated by
5   C&S partners; we are responsible for high-quality work for our clients with very little in-
6   tervening guidance from other accountants in the firm. We felt her candidacy was just too
7   risky. There was also some question about her ability to attract and keep clients, but that
8   was not the controlling issue.
9
10   Paul Buckner was not the deciding force at the meeting. I really don't remember anything
11   he had to say, other than he was abstaining on the Ahmed vote. I don't recall him saying
12   anything about the work Ms. Ahmed did for him on the NCW case of the previous year, but
13   his comments of the previous year were a matter of record.
14
15   His abstaining really didn't have any effect on the outcome of the meeting. Because Paul was
16   the chair, he would have voted only in the case of a tie and the vote on Ms. Ahmed, although
17   it was close, was not a tie. I guess it is possible some partners might have drawn a negative
18   inference from Buckner's abstention, but that didn't seem to be Buckner's purpose. I think
19   he was embarrassed by the whole thing and abstained from voting to rise above the fray.
20   I suppose it was not his most shining hour. He should know better than to have sexual rela-
21   tions with a professional in the firm, especially one who was working directly under him.
22   He knows it. The whole firm knows it. I hope this is the last time anything like this happens.
23
24   As expected, Bill Weisman was Ms. Ahmed's strongest advocate, but he too recognized the
25   potential for future problems if what we had seen was a pattern for Ms. Ahmed. When we
26   finally voted not to nominate Ms. Ahmed for partnership, Bill tried to get us to agree to
27   give her another year. Most of us could not see how another good year would dispel our
28   concerns about inconsistent performance when faced with personal problems. It was this
29   inconsistency, not Ms. Ahmed's intellect or talent, that was at issue. We then authorized
30   her six months with the firm to find other employment.
31
32   I do not believe Paul Buckner used his substantial influence to harm Ms. Ahmed's part-
33   nership chances. I know for a fact he did not talk to me. On balance, his comments at
34   the partnership nomination meeting were positive towards her, even though they were
35   not glowing. The breakup of the relationship between Ms. Ahmed and Paul was never
36   discussed openly in the meeting, although I'm sure it was on the minds of all of us, to the
37   extent that it shed light on Ms. Ahmed's ability to put personal considerations aside when
38   working on her accounting responsibilities. I suppose it's possible some of my partners
39   might have thought that, if they voted against Ms. Ahmed, they were doing Paul Buckner
40   a favor, but I doubt that happened. Paul could have easily handled having Ms. Ahmed as a
41   partner if she was so nominated. If that was a problem and did cause some of my partners
42   to view her nomination negatively, I think that would be a legitimate business decision. If a
43   choice had to be made between Ms. Ahmed and Paul Buckner, and it did not happen here
44   in my opinion, the only correct business decision would be in favor of Paul Buckner.

1   Paul did lose some influence in the firm after the dust settled. He was replaced in September
2   of YR-2 as chair of the audit section, before the end of the normal five-year term. The
3   official statement was that he was stepping down because of his heavy schedule, but it
4   would have been a good decision to get him out of a position of evaluating accountants
5   if there was the potential of personal relationships developing between Paul and women
6   accountants. This is especially so given the fact that Ms. Ahmed filed a complaint against the
7   accounting firm with the EEOC in the summer of YR-2. We issued a general denial at the time
8   and the next thing we knew, the EEOC notified us they had issued a "right to sue" letter to
9   Ms. Ahmed based on the passage of 180 days. As a result, this lawsuit is not a surprise.
10
11   One other fallout from this matter was that the firm lost Bill Weisman as a partner. Appar-
12   ently, Bill and Paul had a falling out about some recommendation letters Paul sent out for
13   Ms. Ahmed. This fact weighed heavily in favor, at least according to him, in Bill accepting a
14   corporate position with NCW. His loss is a substantial one for the firm.
15
16   I understand Ms. Ahmed ended up taking a position on the faculty at the University of Nita
17   Law School as what they call a Practice Professor, teaching accounting for lawyers. She
18   certainly has the intellect for the job, and I'm sure she will succeed if she puts her mind to
19   it. A lot of the talent she displayed for audit should transfer over well to teaching.

I have read this deposition and it is complete and accurate.

Danielle Reddick
Danielle Reddick

Subscribed and sworn before me this 12th day of July, YR-0.

Harry Gibbons
Harry Gibbons
Certified Shorthand Reporter

This deposition was taken in the office of the counsel for the defendants on July 1,
YR-0. This deposition was given under oath and was read and signed by the deponent.

STATEMENT OF MARY LANGFORD

1   My name is Mary Langford. I am forty years old and work for the accounting firm of Cooper
2   & Stewart. My job is as the staff assistant for Paul Buckner, one of the senior partners in
3   the firm. I live at 14 Fells Park Lane in Nita City with my spouse Casey, who is an accountant
4   with the city government, and our child, Cameron, who is twelve years old. We have been
5   married for seventeen years. I have an associate degree in business from Nita Community
6   College, which I obtained by attending school part time while I was working as a clerk at
7   the Drury Plumbing Company after graduating from Nita West High School.
8
9   I have been employed by Cooper & Stewart for twenty years. I joined the firm as a mem-
10 ber of the word processing pool after receiving my associate degree in that same year. In
11 YR-16, I was promoted to work for Paul Buckner as his personal secretary. Mr. Buckner
12 chose me as his secretary when his former secretary left the firm to attend business school.
13 I have worked for Mr. Buckner ever since then. In YR-6, at Mr. Buckner's insistence, I was
14 given the title of senior administrative assistant. This promotion was made to accurately
15 reflect the tasks I performed for Mr. Buckner and meant a substantial raise for me. My cur-
16 rent salary is $56,000 per year. I also receive a small bonus of two to three thousand dollars
17 at the end of each year.
18
19 My job duties for Mr. Buckner include supervising the three clerks who work for Mr. Buck-
20 ner: Cary Jones, John Watters, and Michelle Johns. Mr. Buckner insists all documents for
21 engagements that he heads be prepared by myself or his clerical staff. We are generally re-
22 garded as the top support group in the firm. Cary, John, and Michelle were recruited from
23 other staff assistants within the firm.
24
25 My other duties as Mr. Buckner's senior administrative assistant include keeping his cal-
26 endar, making all his travel arrangements, handling his expense account, dealing with the
27 accountants and staff assistants on his engagement teams, and occasionally going on the
28 road with Mr. Buckner when he needs administrative services that cannot be handled from
29 a distance. In recent years, my travel time has been limited due to the ability to use elec-
30 tronic communication systems that make it easy and efficient to take care of Mr. Buckner's
31 needs from my office at Cooper & Stewart.
32
33 Keeping Mr. Buckner's calendar includes scheduling meetings, confirming telephone con-
34 ference dates, arranging for coverage for matters Mr. Buckner cannot personally attend,
35 and generally being sure Mr. Buckner's time is used efficiently. I also coordinate the engage-
36 ment calendar for other accountants and staff assistants who are working with Mr. Buckner.
37 This oftentimes involves synchronizing with the clerical staff who perform similar tasks for
38 other accountants on the team. As a result, I am aware of the staffing for all engagements
39 and the travel schedules for those other professionals working for and with Mr. Buckner.
40
41 Part of keeping Mr. Buckner's calendar includes making his extensive travel arrangements.
42 He always flies first-class and prefers an aisle seat with the adjoining seat being unoccupied

1   or occupied by the other professional most important to the purpose for which he is travel-
2   ing. For example, if Mr. Buckner is scheduled to be at a client conference, he wants to be
3   seated next to the accountant who can provide information about the engagement that is
4   not apparent from the client's written materials and records. I also make all hotel reserva-
5   tions for Mr. Buckner's business travel because I know the hotels he prefers in most of the
6   major cities in the country, and the restaurants where he likes to eat. Mr. Buckner insists
7   on staying only in hotels where the windows open, and in some hotels he prefers particular
8   suites. These become the work center for the engagement, so a certain level of comfort
9   and convenience is essential. I also handle Mr. Buckner's nonbusiness travel—his prefer-
10   ences for pleasure travel are the same as for business.
11
12   I also handle Mr. Buckner's expense accounts. Mr. Buckner has two American Express cards,
13   one used predominantly for client matters and one used for personal expenses. It is my job
14   to bill the appropriate client for the various charges on Mr. Buckner's bill for his business
15   card, which is paid by the firm. I maintain Mr. Buckner's personal checking account for him;
16   as part of that process I write checks for his signature from his personal account. From
17   time to time, however, a business charge will end up on his personal account or a personal
18   charge will end up on his business account. It is my job to make sure these charges are
19   separated and paid by the appropriate party; a client, the firm, or Mr. Buckner personally.
20
21   Because my job is to assist Mr. Buckner in all matters that can make him most efficient,
22   I will also handle personal matters for him. As I already mentioned, I deal with his personal
23   credit card bills and his personal checking account. I will also, at Mr. Buckner's direction,
24   make purchases for him that might include such things as clothing necessary for travel,
25   gifts for his family or others, or tickets to musical shows, plays, or sporting events.
26
27   When making any travel, hotel, dining, or entertainment arrangement for Mr. Buckner,
28   I always verify whether the arrangement is for a business or personal matter. In that way
29   I can make the appropriate charges to clients or know the nature of certain charges when
30   paying his personal charge bills without taking up Mr. Buckner's valuable time.
31
32   As I've said, I have been working for the firm for twenty years and for Mr. Buckner for sixteen
33   years. I am aware of Mr. Buckner's reputation as a womanizer. I can say, because of my job
34   as his staff assistant, that the rumors are grossly overstated. When I first started work at
35   C&S, I was twenty years old and in the word processing pool, which was one of the firm's
36   primary rumor mills—even now, when most of us are assigned to specific accountants, the
37   clerical staff is awash with breakroom gossiping. Mr. Buckner was often mentioned as hav-
38   ing a reputation for sexual relationships with woman accountants and staff assistants in the
39   firm. I'm sure most of the rumors were just that. Mr. Buckner was, even when I first joined
40   the firm, known as one of the best, busiest, and hardest working accountants in the firm. If
41   he had as many affairs as were rumored, he would have had time for little else.
42
43   While working in the pool, I did several assignments for Mr. Buckner. He was always very
44   friendly to me and took the time to compliment my work and inquire about me as a person.

1   He would comment from time to time that I looked nice, and he never failed to notice a
2   new outfit or haircut. I suppose some would call it flirting, but to me it was just friendly
3   and caring. Mr. Buckner is also a physical person, meaning he talks with his hands and
4   when speaking to someone is likely to put a hand on the other person's arm or shoulder.
5   I never viewed this as sexual in nature, especially because he was the same way with both
6   men and women and remains the same today. He is just as likely to put his hand or arm
7   on the shoulder of John Watters as Cary Jones, both of whom do clerical work for him.
8   I was raised in an Italian family. My maiden name is Rizzo. My family, relatives, and oth-
9   ers in my neighborhood are also physical in the same way. In fact, I have often joked with
10   Mr. Buckner, that he must really be Italian, given the way he acts and talks and his prefer-
11   ence for Italian restaurants.
12
13   Mr. Buckner has never made any sexual advances towards me or any other employees in
14   the pool that I saw, although a couple of the women in the pool were really attracted to
15   him. He knew I was going with Casey, my soon-to-be spouse, because he was interested in
16   me enough to ask me some harmless questions about my personal life. When he wasn't in
17   a big hurry, which was unusual, and could stop and talk, Mr. Buckner would always ask me
18   how Casey was doing, which was nice. He would kid me that he hoped Casey knew what
19   a good thing he had. I always assured Mr. Buckner, that if he knew what was good for him,
20   he did. Mr. Buckner would usually comment something like, "good for him, smart man."
21   I viewed these comments as nothing more than friendly banter, which is what it was. Mr.
22   Buckner was always kind to me and, although he couldn't attend our wedding in YR-17
23   because he was out of town on an engagement, he sent a lovely note and a beautiful crys-
24   tal vase, which we still have.
25
26   As I said earlier, I became Mr. Buckner's personal secretary in YR-16. By that time, there were
27   enough younger accountants in the firm who were comfortable with computers that we
28   didn't need a word processing pool anymore. Instead, most the clerical staff was assigned
29   to individual accountants, with a handful who remained as "floaters." My duties then were
30   about the same as they are now, but on a smaller scale. I was Mr. Buckner's only secretary, al-
31   though we could call on the services of the floating secretaries. Mr. Buckner was just as busy,
32   and I did whatever I could to make his life less hectic. In my first year with him, I volunteered
33   to take over his expense account reports, and I even suggested that he obtain two credit
34   cards to help separate business from personal expenses. About this same time, Mr. Buckner
35   also asked if I would handle his personal checking account, which I was glad to do.
36
37   In working every day with Mr. Buckner, it became clear to me that he was married to his
38   work. He had little time for his family. He always said he needed to find more time for his
39   kids, but he was so much in demand by our clients that he was hardly ever in town more
40   than two weeks in a row; even then, he worked long hours at the office. It also was clear
41   that Mr. Buckner and his wife were not close. Mrs. Buckner would call from time to time
42   to leave messages that Mr. Buckner was to meet her at some event or another, but never
43   asked to speak with him. To be honest, even though he was a huge success on the job,
44   Mr. Buckner always seemed sort of sad to me.

1   Because I was responsible for all of Mr. Buckner's scheduling—making reservations,
2   coordination with other accountants and staff assistants, and dealing with his personal
3   and business finances—I became aware that Mr. Buckner would from time to time, have
4   an affair with one of the women accountants or staff assistants he was working with. The
5   affairs were usually of the same sort. They began after Mr. Buckner and the woman were
6   working intensely on a case, last for the duration of the case, and then end. Contrary to
7   the rumor mill, there weren't a lot of them, and when so involved, Mr. Buckner didn't see
8   other women. I would say that if Mr. Buckner had more than one of these relationships in
9   any eighteen-month period it would be unusual.
10

11   I would know about these relationships, mainly from my job duties. Mr. Buckner never hid
12   them from me, nor did he flaunt the relationships to me or anyone else. He is a very gener-
13   ous man. I could tell a relationship had begun because there would be travel arrangements
14   where he would insist the woman involved travel with him for the duration of the case.
15   There would also be flowers purchased and gifts sent. I believe these relationships were a
16   way for Mr. Buckner to ease the stress of the job, given they hardly ever lasted more than
17   the duration of the engagement. When the relationship ended, Mr. Buckner would usu-
18   ally seem sad for a brief period, and then resume his breakneck work pace and be his old,
19   charming self. I don't condone these relationships, but I can understand them. Mr. Buckner
20   was obviously in a very bad marriage, and this was his way of dealing with it.
21

22   Even though I was aware of these relationships, I tried to respect the privacy of both
23   Mr. Buckner and the woman involved. I never participated in office gossip, except from
24   time to time when I couldn't help myself and responded to some stupid statement about
25   Mr. Buckner to say the person didn't know what they were talking about. But even that
26   was unusual. I took no special interest in these relationships and, except for the relation-
27   ships with Ms. Merritt (which was about ten years ago) and Ms. Ahmed (which happened
28   two years ago), I cannot even recall the names of the women involved.
29

30   Ms. Merritt and Ms. Ahmed were different; both those relationships were serious. I believe
31   Mr. Buckner sincerely loved both women and, but for his commitment to his children,
32   would have divorced his wife and married either one of them. I believe this because of
33   comments Mr. Buckner made about both women, the way he acted around them, the way
34   he spoke of them (it being unusual for him to say anything about any of his partners), and
35   especially the way he reacted when the relationships ended. In both cases he was truly
36   devastated. I can't point to anything concrete or specific to explain why I believe these two
37   relationships were serious, but knowing Mr. Buckner as well as I do, I'm sure I'm right.
38

39   The only specific thing I remember about the aftermath of Mr. Buckner's relationship with
40   Ms. Merritt was that she got back with her husband, and they moved to Washington, DC.
41   Mr. Buckner was very helpful in Ms. Merritt's obtaining a new position in DC. I know be-
42   cause I typed letters on her behalf for Mr. Buckner and placed phone calls to several firms
43   for Mr. Buckner in response to inquiries about Ms. Merritt. I remember this specifically
44   because at that time Rachel Levin was the staff assistant to Mr. Milton, another accountant

1   in the audit section of the firm who was apparently friendly with Ms. Merritt. Rachel made
2   several disparaging remarks about Mr. Buckner to me. I defended him, of course, and told
3   Rachel how Mr. Buckner was devastated by the breakup but even then helped Ms. Merritt
4   get another position in DC.
5
6   The aftermath of the break-up with Ms. Ahmed was, of course, this lawsuit. I have noth-
7   ing to add about this relationship other than what I've said earlier. I do know Mr. Buckner
8   wrote some letters on her behalf after she was denied partnership, but I did not type them,
9   so I know nothing about their contents. It is not unusual for Mr. Buckner to try to help ac-
10 countants leaving the firm to find other jobs. He's done so many times in the past. I am
11 sure Mr. Buckner did not in any way try to hurt Ms. Ahmed's career. He's not that kind of
12 man, and he would never put his personal life ahead of the good of the firm.
13
14 As I said, I can't remember the specifics of any of Mr. Buckner's other relationships. In addi-
15 tion to not wanting to stick my nose into Mr. Buckner's personal business, there is another
16 reason why my memory is no clearer. About seven years ago Mr. Buckner's youngest son,
17 Spencer, was involved in a serious, life-threatening accident. Mr. and Mrs. Buckner became
18 closer than they had been in years and they went through a period where their relation-
19 ship seemed much better. They traveled more together and spent more time together at
20 home as well. From YR-7 until the relationship with Ms. Ahmed, I am not aware of any re-
21 lationship that Mr. Buckner had with any employee of the firm. I believe that if one existed,
22 for all the reasons I've told you about, I would have known about it. Any other relationship
23 would have been a long time ago, before Ms. Merritt, and I just don't remember the de-
24 tails. The rumors about Mr. Buckner never ended, however, which just goes to show that
25 people often will not let the truth get in the way of stories they tell.

EXPERT REPORTS

ASSESSMENT OF ECONOMIC LOSS IN THE MATTER OF AHMED V. BUCKNER AND C&S

Prepared for Defense Counsel by
Cameron Palmero, PhD
YR-0

Prepared by Jerome Staller, PhD, and Stephanie Thomas, PhD, of the Center For Forensic Economic Studies, Suite 1200, 1608 Walnut Street, Philadelphia, PA 19103, (215) 546-5600.

Updated and revised by Kent Mikkelsen, PhD, and Gale Mosteller, PhD, Economists Incorporated, 2121 K Street N.W., Washington DC 20037, (202) 223-4700

Street NW, Washington, DC 20037, (202) 223-4700

Introduction

This report assesses the economic loss suffered by Kiya Ahmed as a result of alleged gender discrimination and defamation of character, which occurred while she worked at the Defendant accounting firm, Cooper & Stewart (C&S), under the supervision of Defendant Buckner. Her economic loss consists of lost earnings. In reaching these conclusions I have relied on all the pleadings and other discovery in this case, as well as those other sources that are specifically mentioned in this report.

Background

After receiving a bachelor's degree in business from Nita University in YR-19, Ms. Ahmed began her employment in YR-16 as a staff assistant at C&S. In YR-13, she entered an online MBA program at the University of Nita School of Business. Ms. Ahmed continued to work for the Defendant accounting firm as while attending business school, first in her role as a staff assistant and then after her first year of the MBA program as an accounting intern. During this time, she received very good performance reviews from her supervisors. Ms. Ahmed graduated first in her class from business school in YR-9, took and passed the CPA exam, and was offered and accepted a position as staff accountant with C&S. Assigned to the audit section of the firm, she worked in that section from September YR-9 through December YR-3. In June YR-2, Ms. Ahmed was considered for a partnership with the firm, but she was not accepted. She was terminated by the firm, effective December 31, YR-2.

After undergoing a period of psychological trauma brought on by a hostile work environment, Ms. Ahmed was able to accept a part-time teaching position at the University of Nita School of Law. Subsequently she was offered a full-time appointment as a Practice Professor of law in the law school beginning September of YR-1. It is anticipated and assumed in this report that this position will become a tenure-track position. Ms. Ahmed is currently forty-one years old and employed as a Practice Professor of Law at the University of Nita.

Assumptions

The following assumptions were made in estimating the economic loss:

Expected Retirement

In my analysis, I have assumed that the plaintiff will retire at age sixty-five.

Earnings Absent the Alleged Incidents

At the request of counsel, I have provided in my analysis two estimates of economic loss to the plaintiff. Specifically, I have assessed the plaintiff's economic loss as the result of alleged gender discrimination and alleged defamation of character.

Discrimination Case

I have valued the potential economic loss to Plaintiff as the result of alleged gender discrimination. Assuming that the plaintiff did suffer gender discrimination, then her potential earnings absent the discrimination are equal to her potential earnings as a partner at C&S.

According to recent articles in *The American Accountant, The Nita Inquirer*, and the *Nita Business Journal*, it is becoming increasingly difficult for accountants to attain partner status. Partnership offers have dropped off at many large accounting firms, and many firms, including C&S, are now offering permanent senior accountant positions in lieu of traditional equity partnerships historically offered to staff accountants. At C&S, permanent senior accountant positions were offered in YR-1 to two accountants who had not attracted new clientele to the firm. All staff accountants who were eligible for partnership review in YR-3 were offered traditional partnerships by C&S. Because the plaintiff demanded a partnership review, the firm never considered her for a permanent senior accountant position. Given that the plaintiff had not developed and was not likely to develop new business for C&S, I have assumed that she would have been offered, at best, a permanent senior accountant position to begin in YR-2 and received the earnings outlined below:

Permanent Senior Accountant Earnings

Year	Salary
1	$150,000
3	$160,000
5	$170,000

This earnings profile was constructed from a national survey of accountants earnings published in the *Nita Business Journal* in YR-1. I have valued these earnings from YR-1 through YR+24, when the plaintiff would reach age sixty-five.

Defamation Case

I have assumed that the plaintiff did not suffer from gender discrimination, but that her character was defamed, thereby resulting in an economic loss due to an inability to market herself to other firms. The same economic and personal factors limiting her ability at C&S would make her unable to become partner at another accounting firm. These factors would include her own inability to generate business for the firm, a lack of accounting skills, a slow economy, etc. Absent defamation, she would probably have been limited to the associate level with another firm.

According to the information from C&S, permanent senior accountants are paid at the level of a sixth-year associate, with inflationary increases. Plaintiff had finished her sixth year at the time of her partnership decision. Her salary at the time was $130,000 per year. I have assumed that the plaintiff would remain a permanent senior accountant at C&S or at an alternative firm at an initial salary of $130,000 per year. I have valued these earnings from January YR-1 until the plaintiff would reach age sixty-five.

Earnings Growth

Some of my earnings estimates use a profile of average earnings for employees with different levels of experience. I have assigned these to the corresponding years in the plaintiff's earning stream using an inflation factor of 2 percent. To estimate future earnings growth outside the profile period, I use 3 percent, the YR-5–YR-1 average annual growth rate in the Business Sector Compensation Per Hour Index.

Discount Rate

Future earnings have been discounted to their present value using a risk-adjusted discount rate of 4 percent.

Earnings in Mitigation

Despite the alleged gender discrimination and defamation, the plaintiff has secured employment as a law school professor. In the spring of YR-1, the plaintiff taught her first law course as an adjunct professor at the University of Nita School of Law and was paid $30,000. She was then offered a full-time position for the YR-1–YR- academic year as a practice professor in the law school. Plaintiff accepted the position with a starting salary of $110,000 per year.

In late YR-2, the plaintiff was offered a position in the corporate counsel's office of NCW at a starting salary of $125,000. Plaintiff did not accept this position, opting to stay at the law school at a lower salary. Given that a higher paying corporate counsel position was open to the plaintiff, she had the potential to earn higher wages; it was her own decision not to do so. As an aside, the existence of such an offer casts serious doubt as to the economic viability of the defamation claim.

In my analysis, I have provided two estimates of the plaintiff's earnings in mitigation. For the first estimate, I have assumed that the plaintiff would have mitigated her economic loss, given the incident, by accepting the position with NCW at a starting salary of $125,000 per year beginning in January YR-1. Based upon information provided by Cliff Fuller at NCW, I have estimated the plaintiff's potential earnings as follows:

Potential Corporate Counsel Earnings at Nita Computer World

Years as Counsel	Salary
1	$160,000
3	$185,000
5	$210,000

By YR+3, the plaintiff's earnings as a corporate counselor exceed those of a non-equity partner at C&S. Therefore, the earnings offset as of YR+3, so there is no economic loss beyond that point. Plaintiff's earnings as a corporate accountant are greater than those as a permanent senior accountant. Therefore, under the assumption that the plaintiff would have remained a permanent senior accountant absent the incident and currently has the potential to be a corporate accountant, her economic loss would be zero.

In the second estimate of the plaintiff's earnings in mitigation, I have estimated her potential earnings as a Practice Professor of Law. According to her deposition testimony, the plaintiff's full-time practice professor salary is $110,000 per year. I have assumed that the plaintiff will remain in the teaching profession, and that by YR+7 she will be promoted to a full practice professor position with a salary of $180,000 per year. This $180,000 figure is based on data provided by the American Association of Law Schools showing the average annual salaries for teachers in law schools.

I have valued earnings and benefits starting in January YR-3. In YR-2, the plaintiff's salary as an associate at C&S was $130,000 per year.

Tables

Table 1 shows earnings as a permanent senior accountant at C&S to age sixty-five.

Table 2 shows earnings as a long-term associate with another accounting firm to age sixty-five.

Table 3 shows earnings as a corporate counselor to age sixty-five.

Table 4 shows earnings and fringe benefits as a law school professor to age sixty-five.

Summary

As outlined in the Summary Table, the total economic loss to the plaintiff ranges from $0 to $342,797.

Summary Table

Kiya Ahmed

Discrimination Case

Earnings absent the incident

Permanent senior accountant	$3,811,650

Earnings in mitigation

Corporate accountant	$4,471,099
Law school professor	$3,468,853

Total Economic Loss

Corporate accountant	$0
Law school professor	$342,797

Defamation Case

Earnings absent the incident

Permanent senior accountant	$3,183,281

Earnings in mitigation

Corporate accountant	$4,471,099
Law school professor	$3,468,853

Total Economic Loss

Corporate accountant	$0
Law school professor	$0

Table 1

Permanent Senior Accountant at C&S

Year	Age	Profile	In Current Dollars	Discounted to YR-0
YR-2	39		130,000	130,000
YR-1	40	150,000	147,059	147,059
YR-0	41	155,000	155,000	155,000
YR+1	42	160,000	163,200	156,923
YR+2	43	165,000	171,666	158,715
YR+3	44	170,000	180,405	160,380
YR+4	45		185,818	158,838
YR+5	46		191,392	157,310
YR+6	47		197,134	155,798
YR+7	48		203,048	154,300
YR+8	49		209,139	152,816
YR+9	50		215,413	151,347
YR+10	51		221,876	149,891
YR+11	52		228,532	148,450
YR+12	53		235,388	147,023
YR+13	54		242,450	145,609
YR+14	55		249,723	144,209
YR+15	56		257,215	142,822
YR+16	57		264,931	141,449
YR+17	58		272,879	140,089
YR+18	59		281,066	138,742
YR+19	60		289,498	137,408
YR+20	61		298,183	136,087
YR+21	62		307,128	134,778
YR+22	63		316,342	133,482
YR+23	64		325,832	132,199
YR+24	65		335,607	130,928
				3,811,650

Discount rate	4.0%
Inflation rate	2.0%
Wage growth rate	3.0%

Table 2

Long-Term Associate at Another Accounting Firm

Year	Age	Profile	In Current Dollars	Discounted to YR-0
YR-2	39	130,000	130,000	130,000
YR-1	40		133,900	133,900
YR-0	41		137,917	137,917
YR+1	42		140,675	135,265
YR+2	43		144,896	133,964
YR+3	44		149,242	132,676
YR+4	45		153,720	131,400
YR+5	46		158,331	130,137
YR+6	47		163,081	128,886
YR+7	48		167,974	127,646
YR+8	49		173,013	126,419
YR+9	50		178,203	125,203
YR+10	51		183,549	123,999
YR+11	52		189,056	122,807
YR+12	53		194,728	121,626
YR+13	54		200,569	120,457
YR+14	55		206,586	119,299
YR+15	56		212,784	118,151
YR+16	57		219,168	117,015
YR+17	58		225,743	115,890
YR+18	59		232,515	114,776
YR+19	60		239,490	113,672
YR+20	61		246,675	112,579
YR+21	62		254,075	111,497
YR+22	63		261,698	110,425
YR+23	64		269,548	109,363
YR+24	65		277,635	108,311
				3,183,281

Discount rate	4.0%
Inflation rate	2.0%
Wage growth rate	3.0%

Table 3

Corporate Counsel

Year	Age	Profile	In Current Dollars	Discounted to YR-0
YR-2	39		130,000	130,000
YR-1	40		66,667	66,667
YR-0	41	160,000	160,000	160,000
YR+1	42	172,500	175,950	169,183
YR+2	43	185,000	192,474	177,953
YR+3	44	197,500	209,589	186,323
YR+4	45	210,000	227,311	194,306
YR+5	46		234,130	192,438
YR+6	47		241,154	190,587
YR+7	48		248,389	188,755
YR+8	49		255,840	186,940
YR+9	50		263,515	185,142
YR+10	51		271,421	183,362
YR+11	52		279,564	181,599
YR+12	53		287,950	179,853
YR+13	54		296,589	178,124
YR+14	55		305,487	176,411
YR+15	56		314,651	174,715
YR+16	57		324,091	173,035
YR+17	58		333,814	171,371
YR+18	59		343,828	169,723
YR+19	60		354,143	168,091
YR+20	61		364,767	166,475
YR+21	62		375,710	164,874
YR+22	63		386,981	163,289
YR+23	64		398,591	161,719
YR+24	65		410,549	160,164
				4,471,099

Discount rate	4.0%
Inflation rate	2.0%
Wage growth rate	3.0%

Table 4

Law School Professor

Year	Age	Profile	In Current Dollars	Discounted to YR-0
YR-2	39		130,000	130,000
YR-1	40	110,000	66,667	66,667
YR-0	41	110,000	112,200	112,200
YR+1	42	110,000	114,444	110,042
YR+2	43	110,000	116,733	107,926
YR+3	44	110,000	119,068	105,851
YR+4	45	110,000	121,449	103,815
YR+5	46	110,000	123,878	101,819
YR+6	47	110,000	126,355	99,861
YR+7	48	180,000	210,899	160,266
YR+8	49		217,226	158,725
YR+9	50		223,742	157,198
YR+10	51		230,455	155,687
YR+11	52		237,368	154,190
YR+12	53		244,489	152,707
YR+13	54		251,824	151,239
YR+14	55		259,379	149,785
YR+15	56		267,160	148,345
YR+16	57		275,175	146,918
YR+17	58		283,430	145,505
YR+18	59		291,933	144,106
YR+19	60		300,691	142,721
YR+20	61		309,712	141,348
YR+21	62		319,003	139,989
YR+22	63		328,573	138,643
YR+23	64		338,430	137,310
YR+24	65		348,583	135,990
				3,468,853

Discount rate	4.0%
Inflation rate	2.0%
Wage growth rate	3.0%

Discovered Information Relating to Cameron Palmero, PhD (Defendants' Expert)

Answers to interrogatories and other discovery have revealed the following concerning defendants' expert, Dr. Palmero. Note: Defendants are aware that Plaintiff has this information.

Dr. Palmero is forty-three years old and one of the founding members of Forensic Economics, Ltd. in Nita City. She started this business fifteen years ago, with a classmate from Nita University, John Pierce. Both she and Pierce received their PhD degrees from Nita University in YR-20, and after a year of postdoctoral work at the university, founded Forensic Economics, Ltd. They now employ ten economists and fifteen support staff. Their sole business is performing litigation support work for law firms.

Dr. Palmero testifies predominantly for defendants. In recent years she has developed a specialty in working for defense counsel in race, gender, and age discrimination cases. Several of her cases have involved claims for economic loss, due to discrimination, for members of the legal and accounting professions, so she has worked with the economics of the accounting profession in the past.

Dr. Palmero's average fee for each case, including time spent testifying in deposition and trials, is between $9,000 and $10,000. She bills her report preparation time at $350 per hour; her fee for testifying at trial or deposition is $3,000 per day. Dr. Palmero has testified as an expert witness in excess of sixty times in the courts of Nita City (both state and federal). In all but three of those cases she testified as an expert witness for the defendant, in whose interest it was to minimize claimed economic losses.

Cooper & Stewart's attorneys (Speakman and Forman) have retained Dr. Palmero as an expert witness for twenty-five cases in the past ten years. In all those cases, those lawyers represented the defendant in a discrimination case. She has never worked with anyone from C&S in any of those cases. This is the first matter where she has worked with defense counsel Emily Erway of the Speakman firm.

Dr. Palmero has no scholarly publications. She is a frequent speaker, however, in continuing education seminars sponsored by the Nita City and State Bar Associations and the Nita chapter of the American Institute of Certified Public Accountants. She speaks on topics relating to forensic economics and effective methods for presenting such testimony.

Dr. Palmero responded to interrogatories that she recognized Dr. Aki Chau's book, Forensic Economics (5th ed. Nita University Press, 2002), as a generally authoritative source in the area of forensic economics, but did not rely on the text specifically in reaching her opinion in this case. Dr. Chau was a professor at Nita University while Dr. Palmero was both an undergraduate and graduate student. She took a number of courses from him and did well academically, but did not have a close professional relationship—he did not advise her on her thesis or act as a reference for her.

ASSESSMENT OF ECONOMIC LOSS IN THE MATTER OF AHMED V. BUCKNER AND C&S

Prepared for Counsel for the Plaintiff by
Aki Chau, PhD
YR-0

Prepared by Jerome Staller, PhD, and Stephanie Thomas, PhD, of The Center for Forensic Economic Studies, Suite 1200, 1608 Walnut Street, Philadelphia, PA 19103, (215) 546-5600

Updated and revised by Kent Mikkelsen, PhD, and Gale Mosteller, PhD, Economists Incorporated, 2121 K

Street NW, Washington, DC 20037, (202) 223-4700

Introduction

This report assesses the economic loss suffered by Kiya Ahmed as a result of alleged gender discrimination and defamation of character, which occurred while she worked at the Defendant accounting firm, Cooper & Stewart (C&S), under the supervision of Defendant Buckner. Her economic loss consists of lost earnings. In reaching these conclusions, I have relied on all the pleadings and other discovery in this case, as well as those other sources that are specifically mentioned in this report.

Background

After receiving a bachelor's degree in business from Nita University in YR-19, Ms. Ahmed began her employment in YR-16 as a staff assistant at C&S. In YR-13, she entered an online MBA program at the University of Nita School of Business. Ms. Ahmed continued to work for the Defendant accounting firm as while attending business school, first in her role as a staff assistant and then after her first year of the MBA program as an accounting intern. During this time, she received very good performance reviews from her supervisors. Ms. Ahmed graduated first in her class from business school in YR-9, took and passed the CPA exam, and was offered and accepted a position as staff accountant with C&S. Assigned to the audit section of the firm, she worked in that section from September YR-9 through December YR-3. In June YR-2, Ms. Ahmed was considered for a partnership with the firm, but despite excellent work reviews by her supervisors and clients, she was not accepted. She was terminated by the firm, effective December 31, YR-2.

After undergoing a period of psychological trauma brought on by a hostile work environment, Ms. Ahmed was able to accept a part-time teaching position at the University of Nita School of Law. Subsequently she was offered a full-time appointment as a Practice Professor of law in the law school beginning September of YR-1. It is anticipated and assumed in this report that this position will become a tenure-track position. Ms. Ahmed is currently forty-one years old and employed as a Practice Professor of Law at the University of Nita.

Assumptions

I made the following assumptions in estimating the economic loss to Ms. Ahmed:

1) <u>Retirement Age</u>

In this analysis I have assumed that Ms. Ahmed will work until the age of sixty-five.

Potential Earnings Absent Discrimination and Defamation

At counsel's request, I have provided two estimates of the economic loss to Ms. Ahmed. I have assessed Ms. Ahmed's economic loss as a result of the alleged (a) gender discrimination and (b) defamation of character.

Discrimination

I have assumed that the economic loss to Ms. Ahmed is a direct result of the alleged gender discrimination she incurred as an employee at C&S. I have valued her potential earnings absent the discrimination as Ms. Ahmed's potential earnings as a partner at C&S. According to the information received from C&S, their partners have the following earnings pattern:

Earnings of Partners at Cooper & Stewart

Year as Part-ner	Number of Part-ners	Median	Mean	Range
1	4	130,000	127,500	110,000 to 140,000
3	6	160,000	155,000	120,000 to 200,000
5	3	280,000	260,000	200,000 to 300,000
7	4	350,000	356,250	225,000 to 500,000
10	5	460,000	475,000	275,000 to 600,000
20	4	475,000	500,000	300,000 to 750,000

I have assumed that absent discrimination Ms. Ahmed would have become a partner at C&S in January YR-1, and her earnings would have followed the pattern outlined above for mean earnings. I have valued earnings from YR-1 through YR+24, when Ms. Ahmed would reach age sixty-five.

Defamation

I have assumed that Ms. Ahmed did not suffer from gender discrimination, but that defamation of her character resulted in economic loss. Absent defamation, Ms. Ahmed may have secured alternative employment at another accounting firm. However, due to the alleged defamation, she was unable to secure alternative employment at another accounting firm. Her potential earnings absent defamation equal the earnings at an alternative accounting firm. I have assumed that she would have secured such employment as of January 1, YR-1. I have further assumed that she would have remained an associate at the alternative firm until January 1, YR+2 and then would have been promoted to partner. My assumption is that her earnings would have followed the pattern below:

Earnings at Alternative Accounting Firm

Year	Position	Median Earnings
		(YR-0 dollars)
YR-1	Associate	$90,000
YR-0	Associate	100,000
YR+1	Associate	110,000
YR+2	Partner	150,000
YR+4	Partner	175,000
YR+6	Partner	200,000
YR+8	Partner	225,000
YR+11	Partner	250,000
YR+21	Partner	300,000

This earnings pattern has been derived from a national survey of earnings by accountants published in the *Nita Business Journal* in YR-0. In this estimate, I have assumed that Ms. Ahmed's earnings would have been equal to the median earnings for all partners. This is in contrast to potential earnings at C&S, a top-level accounting firm with the earnings to match.

1) Future Growth of Earnings

Earnings growth was estimated as 3.6 percent per year. This rate represents the average annual rate of change in the Compensation Per Hour Index from YR-20 to YR-1.

2) Discount Rate

I have discounted future earnings to their present value. Based on the market yield on U.S. Treasury securities at ten-year constant maturity from January–April YR-0, I have used a nominal rate of 2 percent.

3) Earnings in Mitigation

In the spring of YR-1, Ms. Ahmed became a practice professor at the University of Nita School of Law. She became a member of the full-time faculty in September of YR-1. Her starting salary was $110,000 per year. It is anticipated and assumed in this report that her position will be converted to tenure-track within a year.

I have assumed that Ms. Ahmed will remain in the teaching profession and that by YR+1 she will be promoted to a full professor position with a salary of $160,000 per year. This figure is based upon data from the University of Nita School of Law as to the average annual salaries of full professors.

4) Future Growth and Discounting of Earnings

I have utilized the same growth and discounting methodologies as described earlier.

Tables

Table 1 shows earnings as a partner at C&S to age sixty-five.

Table 2 shows earnings as an associate/partner at an alternative accounting firm to age sixty-five.

Table 3 shows earnings as a law professor to age sixty-five.

Summary

As outlined in the Summary Table, the total economic loss to Ms. Ahmed ranges from $2,542,231 to $8,384,386.

SUMMARY TABLE

KIYA AHMED

DISCRIMINATION

Earnings Absent the Incident	$12,935,991
Less:	
Earnings Given the Incident	$4,551,605
Total Economic Loss	$8,384,386

DEFAMATION

Earnings Absent the Incident	$7,093,836
Less:	
Earnings Given the Incident	$4,551,605
Total Economic Loss	$2,542,231

Table 1
Earnings as a Partner at C&S

Year	Age	YR-0 Profile	Current Dollars	Discounted to YR-0
YR-1	40		130,000	130,000
YR-0	41		134,680	134,680
YR+1	42	155,000	160,580	157,431
YR+2	43		166,361	159,901
YR+3	44	260,000	289,103	272,428
YR+4	45		299,511	276,702
YR+5	46	356,250	425,161	385,082
YR+6	47		440,467	391,122
YR+7	48		456,324	397,257
YR+8	49	475,000	630,335	537,985
YR+9	50		653,027	546,424
YR+10	51		676,536	554,995
YR+11	52		700,892	563,701
YR+12	53		726,124	572,544
YR+13	54		752,264	581,525
YR+14	55		779,346	590,647
YR+15	56		807,402	599,912
YR+16	57		836,469	609,322
YR+17	58		866,582	618,880
YR+18	59	500,000	945,030	661,672
YR+19	60		979,051	672,051
YR+20	61		1,014,297	682,593
YR+21	62		1,050,812	693,300
YR+22	63		1,088,641	704,175
YR+23	64		1,127,832	715,221
YR+24	65		1,168,434	726,440
				12,935,991

Wage growth rate = 3.6 percent

Discount rate = 2.0 percent

Table 2

Earnings as a Partner at Alternative Accounting Firm

Year	Age	YR-0 Profile	Current Dollars	Discounted to YR-0
YR-1	40	90,000	86,873	86,873
YR-0	41	100,000	100,000	100,000
YR+1	42	110,000	113,960	111,725
YR+2	43	150,000	160,994	154,743
YR+3	44		166,790	157,170
YR+4	45	175,000	201,594	186,241
YR+5	46		208,851	189,163
YR+6	47	200,000	247,280	219,577
YR+7	48		256,182	223,022
YR+8	49	225,000	298,580	254,835
YR+9	50		309,329	258,832
YR+10	51		320,465	262,893
YR+11	52	250,000	368,890	296,685
YR+12	53		382,170	301,339
YR+13	54		395,929	306,066
YR+14	55		410,182	310,867
YR+15	56		424,949	315,743
YR+16	57		440,247	320,696
YR+17	58		456,096	325,726
YR+18	59		472,515	330,836
YR+19	60		489,526	336,025
YR+20	61		507,148	341,296
YR+21	62	300,000	630,487	415,980
YR+22	63		653,185	422,505
YR+23	64		676,699	429,133
YR+24	65		701,060	435,864
				7,093,836

Wage growth rate = 3.6%
Discount rate = 2.0%

Table 3

Earnings as a Law Professor

Year	Age	YR-0 Profile	Current Dollars	Discounted to YR-0
YR-1	40	110,000	66,667	66,667
YR-0	41		110,000	110,000
YR+1	42		113,960	111,725
YR+2	43		118,063	113,478
YR+3	44		122,313	115,258
YR+4	45		126,716	117,066
YR+5	46		131,278	118,902
YR+6	47	160,000	136,004	120,768
YR+7	48		204,945	178,417
YR+8	49		212,323	181,216
YR+9	50		219,967	184,059
YR+10	51		227,886	186,946
YR+11	52		236,090	189,878
YR+12	53		244,589	192,857
YR+13	54		253,394	195,882
YR+14	55		262,516	198,955
YR+15	56		271,967	202,076
YR+16	57		281,758	205,245
YR+17	58		291,901	208,465
YR+18	59		302,410	211,735
YR+19	60		313,296	215,056
YR+20	61		324,575	218,430
YR+21	62		336,260	221,856
YR+22	63		348,365	225,336
YR+23	64		360,906	228,871
YR+24	65		373,899	232,461

4,551,605

Wage growth rate = 3.6%
Discount rate = 2.0%

DISCOVERED INFORMATION RELATING TO AKI CHAU, PHD (PLAINTIFF'S EXPERT)

Answers to interrogatories and other discovery have revealed the following concerning Plaintiff's expert, Dr. Chau. Note: Plaintiff is aware that Defendants have this information.

Dr. Chau is fifty-two years old and the Chair of the Department of Economics at Nita University. He obtained his PhD in economics in YR-23 from the University of Pennsylvania and has been employed as a professor at Nita University since then. Dr. Chau received tenure in YR-20, a year earlier than normal, and was promoted to full professor three years later. In YR-17 he was named the Charles Burkett Professor of Economics, the most important chair in the Economics Department at Nita University. He has been the chair of the Economics Department for the past eight years.

Dr. Chau has written over 100 books and articles in his career. He is the author of a book entitled FORENSIC ECONOMICS, which is generally regarded as a leading text in the field. It is used at over 100 universities around the world as the standard text on the topic of forensic economics. The book was originally published in YR-21 by Nita University Press and is currently in its fifth edition.

Dr. Chau does not testify regularly as an expert witness. His last appearance as an expert was eight years ago when he appeared on behalf of a colleague in the university who was seriously injured in an automobile accident. His professional life is geared toward the academic study of economics, and he does not have an active consulting business that would lead him to serve as an expert witness with any regularity. He claims no particular expertise in the economics of the accounting profession; he views it as a part of the service sector of the economy.

Dr. Chau does not know Ms. Ahmed personally, except for his interaction with her in this case. He agreed to testify on her behalf after his good friend, Dean Martin Purcell of the Nita University School of Law, asked him to do so. Ms. Ahmed is employed as a Practice Professor of Law.

Dr. Chau was an instructor at Nita University while Dr. Williamson (the defendant's expert) was both an undergraduate and graduate student. He recalls that she was a good student, but not an outstanding one.

Dr. Chau was recently turned down for a large grant made by the Cooper Foundation, which is named for one of the founding partners of C&S. The foundation is managed by the C&S accounting firm. The $750,000 grant, which was made instead to Dr. Harriet Graham of Nita State University, was for a three-year study on predicting wage growth patterns in service industries for the next twenty years. Dr. Chau and Dr. Graham were the finalists for the grant.

EXHIBITS

Kiya Ahmed

kahmed@nitamail.nita

819-555-3475

Profile

Licensed CPA with nine years experience in financial audits and forensic accounting. Experience reviewing accounting for legal cases and preparing for expert testimony.

Skills

Oracle NetSuite

Microsoft Azure

VMware

SageIntacct

Microsoft Office

Employment History

Practice Professor/University of Nita School of Law

December YR-1–Present

Teaching accounting principles to law students.
Courses taught: Accounting for Lawyers, Forensic Accounting, Forensic Accounting in Complex Antitrust Litigation

CPA Certified Accountant/Cooper & Stewart

YR-9–YR-2

Worked on the full range of auditing matters. Research, audit analysis, preparation for audits, forensic accounting, assisting in preparation of trial counsel for deposition and trial practice, including written preparation of auditing issues and analysis utilized in motion practice, deposition and trial, and appeal.

Accountant Assistant/Cooper & Stewart

YR-12–YR-9

Performed support duties for accountants, including research, audit preparation, trial support, and tax preparation.

Education

University of Nita, MBA YR-9

Honors: Summa Cum Laude
        Mary & William Walsh Award for Scholarship
        Thomas Knox Award for Excellence in Writing

University of Nita, BA, Business Administration, YR-19

Honors: Phi Beta Kappa

Licensure

Certified Public Accountant, YR-9

Publication

FORENSIC ACCOUNTING IN MULTI-PARTY ANTITRUST LITIGATION, 58 Conwell U. L. Rev, YR-1.

COOPER & STEWART

Four Independence Square
Nita City, Nita 57816
819.555.3458

July 1, YR-9

Ms. Kiya Ahmed
Cooper & Stewart
Four Independence Square
Nita City, Nita 57816

Dear Ms. Ahmed,

This letter confirms that you have accepted a position with the accounting firm of Cooper & Stewart as a CPA Accountant, to work predominantly in the audit section. Your beginning annual salary will be $85,000.00.

You will be required to assume the normal responsibilities of a CPA Accountant with the firm, and it is understood that your position with the firm will be evaluated each year.

As you are currently employed as an accounting assistant, you are familiar with the benefits package at C&S, so I will not cover them specifically in this letter. If you have any questions concerning our benefits package, please contact Mary Williamson in our benefits office. As you know, you will receive one month's salary to compensate you for your time spent in studying for the CPA examination.

Please notify me at your earliest convenience as to your anticipated starting date with the firm. We look forward to your coming on board.

If the above terms and conditions are acceptable to you, please indicate same by signing and returning one copy of this letter.

Sincerely,

Charles Milton, Chair
Audits Group

Signed: _____
Kiya Ahmed
Date: 7-10-YR-9

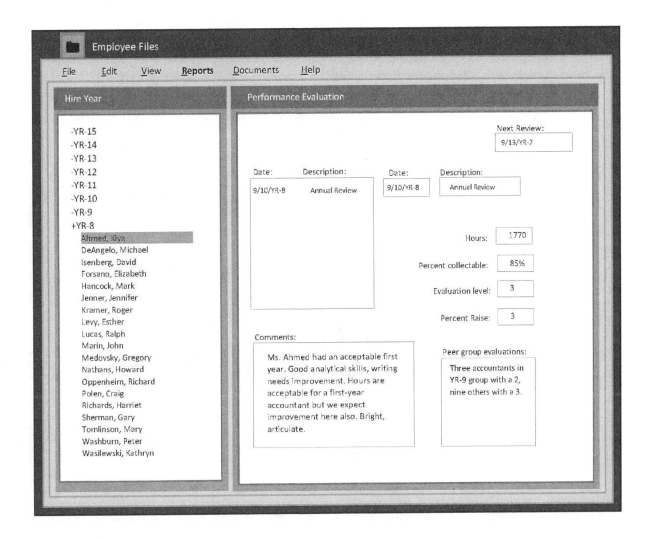

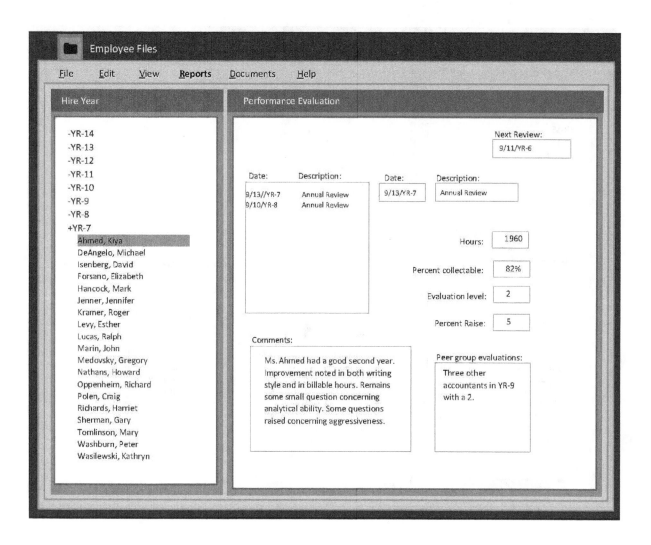

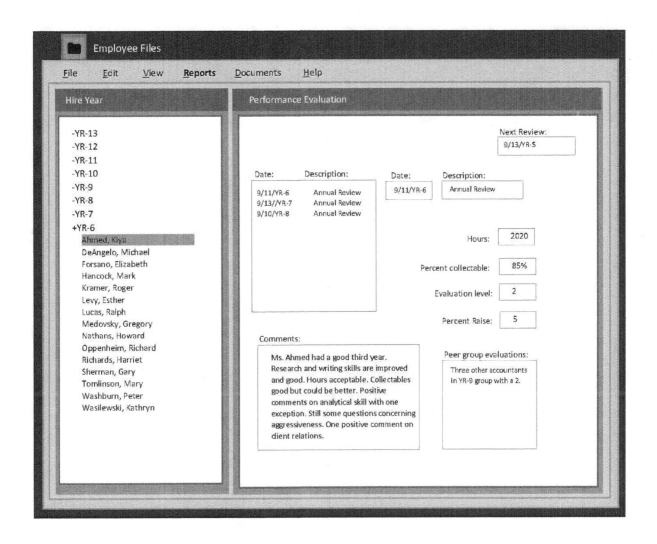

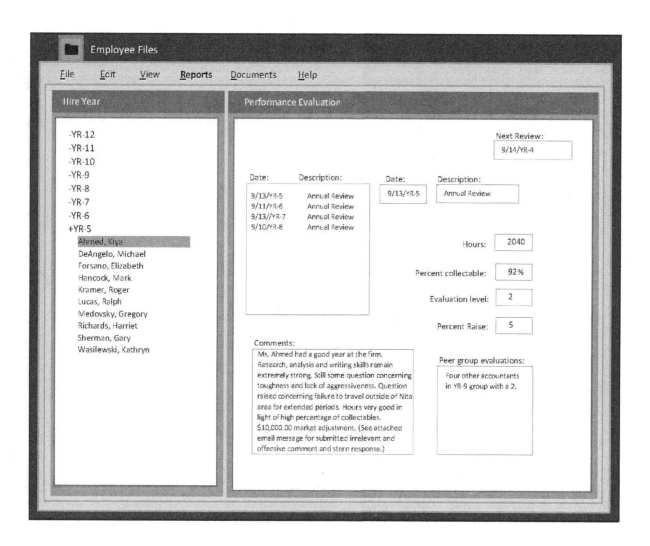

Employee Files

File   Edit   View   **Reports**   Documents   Help

Hire Year | Performance Evaluation

-YR-12
-YR-11
-YR-10
-YR-9
-YR-8
-YR-7
-YR-6
+YR-5
Ahmed, Kiya
DeAngelo, Michael
Forsano, Elizabeth
Hancock, Mark
Kramer, Roger
Lucas, Ralph
Medovsky, Gregory
Richards, Harriet
Sherman, Gary
Wasilewski, Kathryn

Next Review:
9/14/YR-4

Date: Description: Date: Description:
9/13/YR-5   Annual Review   9/13/YR-5   Annual Review
9/11/YR-6   Annual Review
9/13//YR-7   Annual Review
9/10/YR-8   Annual Review

Hours: 2040

Percent collectable: 92%

Evaluation level: 2

Percent Raise: 5

Comments:
Ms. Ahmed had a good year at the firm.
Research, analysis and writing skills remain
extremely strong. Still some question concerning
toughness and lack of aggressiveness. Question
raised concerning failure to travel outside of Nita
area for extended periods. Hours very good in
light of high percentage of collectables.
$10,000.00 market adjustment. (See attached
email message for submitted irrelevant and
offensive comment and stern response.)

Peer group evaluations:
Four other accountants
in YR-9 group with a 2.

Exhibit 3D-1

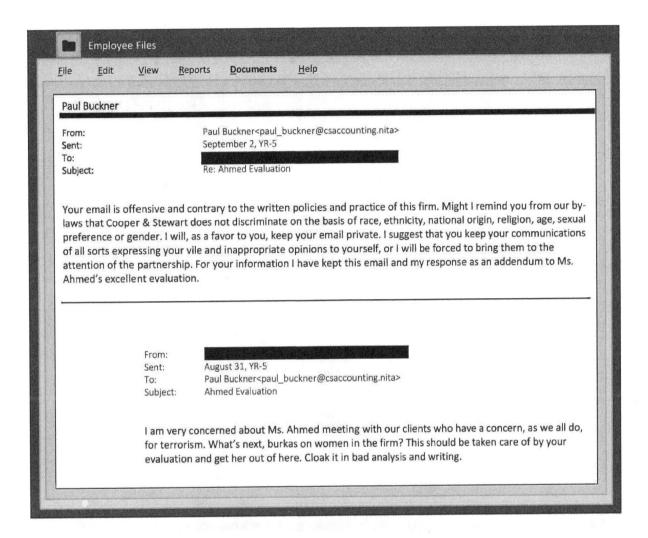

Employee Files

File   Edit   View   Reports   **Documents**   Help

Paul Buckner

From: Paul Buckner<paul_buckner@csaccounting.nita>
Sent: September 2, YR-5
To: ▬▬▬▬▬▬▬▬▬▬
Subject: Re: Ahmed Evaluation

Your email is offensive and contrary to the written policies and practice of this firm. Might I remind you from our by-laws that Cooper & Stewart does not discriminate on the basis of race, ethnicity, national origin, religion, age, sexual preference or gender. I will, as a favor to you, keep your email private. I suggest that you keep your communications of all sorts expressing your vile and inappropriate opinions to yourself, or I will be forced to bring them to the attention of the partnership. For your information I have kept this email and my response as an addendum to Ms. Ahmed's excellent evaluation.

From: ▬▬▬▬▬▬▬▬▬▬
Sent: August 31, YR-5
To: Paul Buckner<paul_buckner@csaccounting.nita>
Subject: Ahmed Evaluation

I am very concerned about Ms. Ahmed meeting with our clients who have a concern, as we all do, for terrorism. What's next, burkas on women in the firm? This should be taken care of by your evaluation and get her out of here. Cloak it in bad analysis and writing.

Exhibit 3E

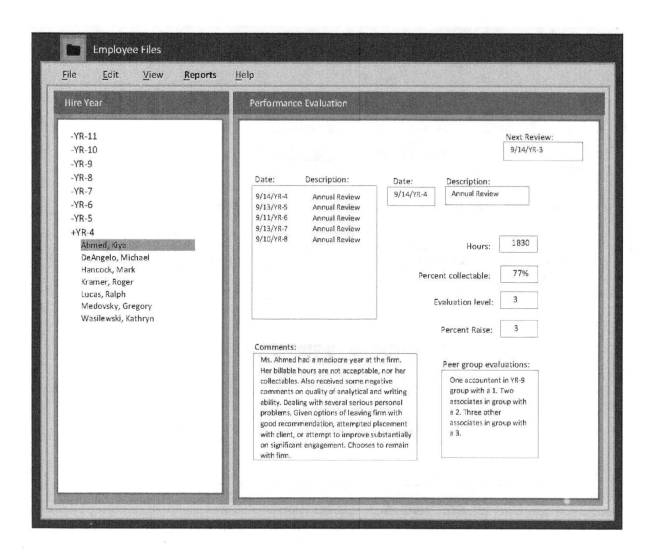

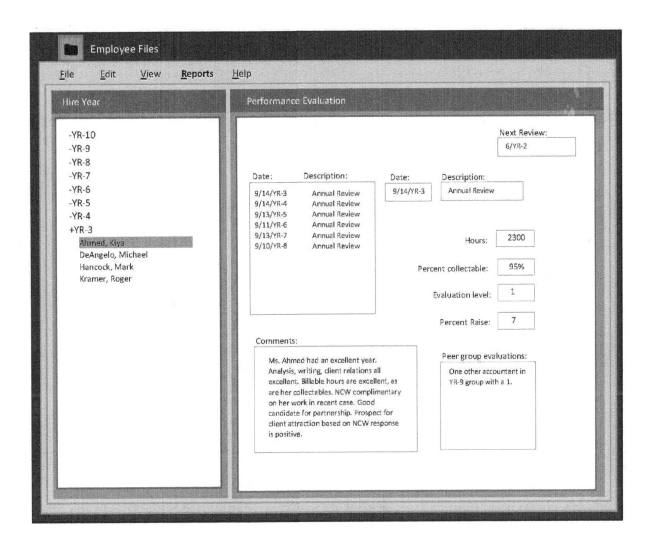

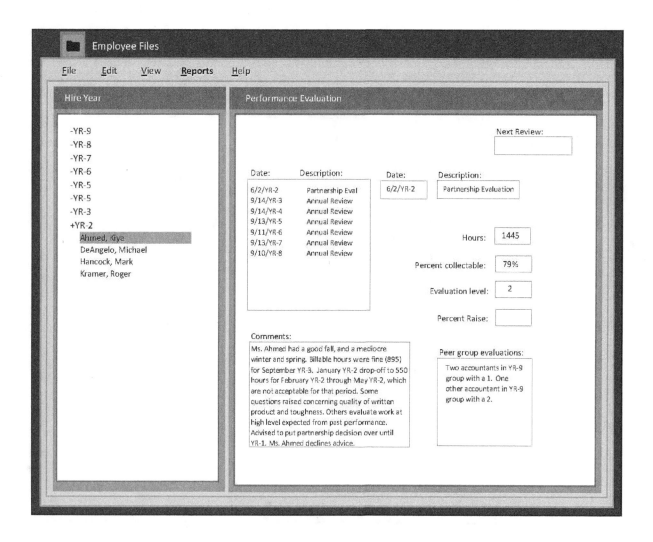

Employee Files

File Edit View **Reports** Help

Hire Year

- -YR-9
- -YR-8
- -YR-7
- -YR-6
- -YR-5
- -YR-5
- -YR-3
- +YR-2
  - Ahmed, Kiya
  - DeAngelo, Michael
  - Hancock, Mark
  - Kramer, Roger

Performance Evaluation

Next Review:

Date:	Description:
6/2/YR-2	Partnership Eval
9/14/YR-3	Annual Review
9/14/YR-4	Annual Review
9/13/YR-5	Annual Review
9/11/YR-6	Annual Review
9/13/YR-7	Annual Review
9/10/YR-8	Annual Review

Date: 6/2/YR-2   Description: Partnership Evaluation

Hours: 1445

Percent collectable: 79%

Evaluation level: 2

Percent Raise:

Comments:

Ms. Ahmed had a good fall, and a mediocre winter and spring. Billable hours were fine (895) for September YR-3. January YR-2 drop-off to 550 hours for February YR-2 through May YR-2, which are not acceptable for that period. Some questions raised concerning quality of written product and toughness. Others evaluate work at high level expected from past performance. Advised to put partnership decision over until YR-1. Ms. Ahmed declines advice.

Peer group evaluations:

Two accountants in YR-9 group with a 1. One other accountant in YR-9 group with a 2.

COOPER & STEWART

Four Independence Square
Nita City, Nita 57816
819.555.3458

September 20, YR-8

Ms. Kiya Ahmed
Cooper & Stewart
Four Independence Square
Nita City, Nita 57816

Dear Ms. Ahmed:

This is to confirm that your salary for the year September YR-8 through September YR-7 will be $87,550.00. This represents a merit raise of 3 percent.

Your contributions to the firm are appreciated.

Sincerely,

Charles Milton
Chair, Audit Group

COOPER & STEWART

Four Independence Square
Nita City, Nita 57816
819.555.3458

September 22, YR-7

Ms. Kiya Ahmed
Cooper & Stewart
Four Independence Square
Nita City, Nita 57816

Dear Ms. Ahmed,

This is to confirm that your salary for the year September YR-7 through September YR-6 will be $91,928.00. This represents a merit raise of 5 percent.

Your contributions to the firm are appreciated.

Sincerely,

Charles Milton
Chair, Audit Group

COOPER & STEWART

Four Independence Square
Nita City, Nita 57816
819.555.3458

September 18, YR-6

Ms. Kiya Ahmed
Cooper & Stewart
Four Independence Square
Nita City, Nita 57816

Dear Ms. Ahmed,

This is to confirm that your salary for the year September YR-6 through September YR-5 will be $96,525.00. This represents a merit raise of 5 percent.

Your contributions to the firm are appreciated.

Sincerely,

Charles Milton
Chair, Audit Group

Exhibit 4D

COOPER & STEWART
Four Independence Square
Nita City, Nita 57816
819.555.3458

September 21, YR-5

Ms. Kiya Ahmed
Cooper & Stewart
Four Independence Square
Nita City, Nita 57816

Dear Ms. Ahmed,

This is to confirm that your salary for the year September YR-5 through September YR-4 will be $111,352.00. This represents a merit raise of 5 percent and a market adjustment of $10,000.00.

Your contributions to the firm are appreciated.

Sincerely,

Paul Buckner

Paul Buckner
Chair, Audit Group

COOPER & STEWART

Four Independence Square
Nita City, Nita 57816
819.555.3458

September 22, YR-4

Ms. Kiya Ahmed
Cooper & Stewart
Four Independence Square
Nita City, Nita 57816

Dear Ms. Ahmed,

This is to confirm that your salary for the year September YR-4 through September YR-3 will be $114,693.00. This represents a merit raise of 3 percent.

The firm values your contributions and we look forward to a productive year.

Sincerely,

Paul Buckner

Paul Buckner
Chair, Audit Group

COOPER & STEWART

Four Independence Square
Nita City, Nita 57816
819.555.3458

September 24, YR-3

Ms. Kiya Ahmed
Cooper & Stewart
Four Independence Square
Nita City, Nita 57816

Dear Ms. Ahmed,

This is to confirm that your salary for the year September YR-3 through September YR-2 will be $122,721. This represents a merit raise of 7 percent.

The firm values your contributions and we look forward to a productive year.

Warm Regards,

Paul Buckner

Paul Buckner
Chair, Audit Group

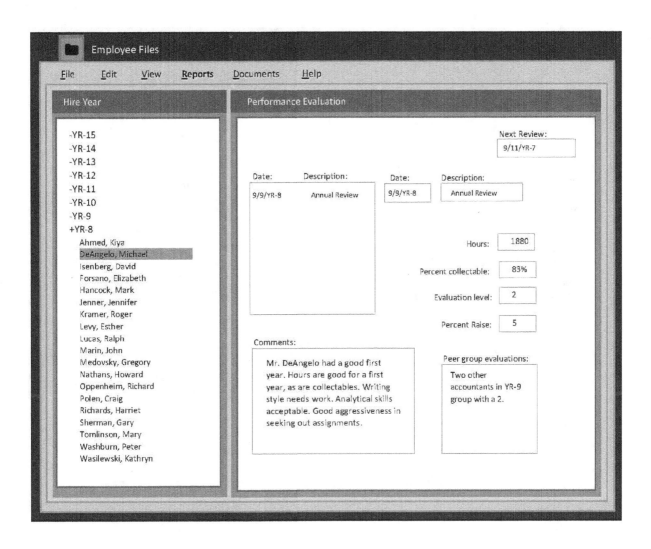

Exhibit 5B

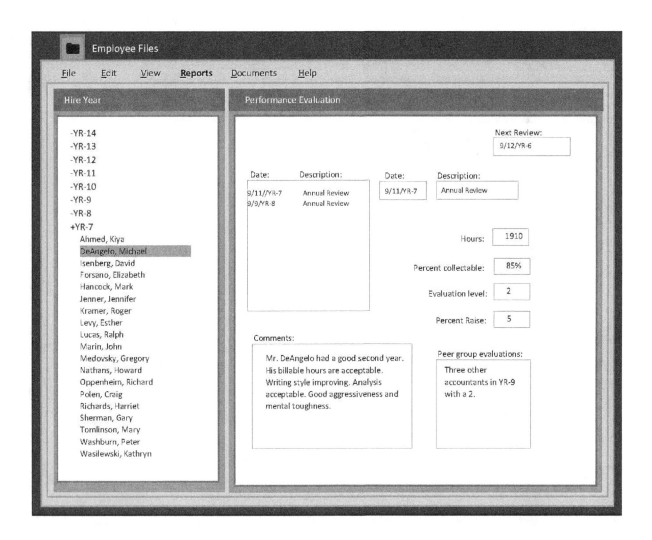

Exhibit 5C

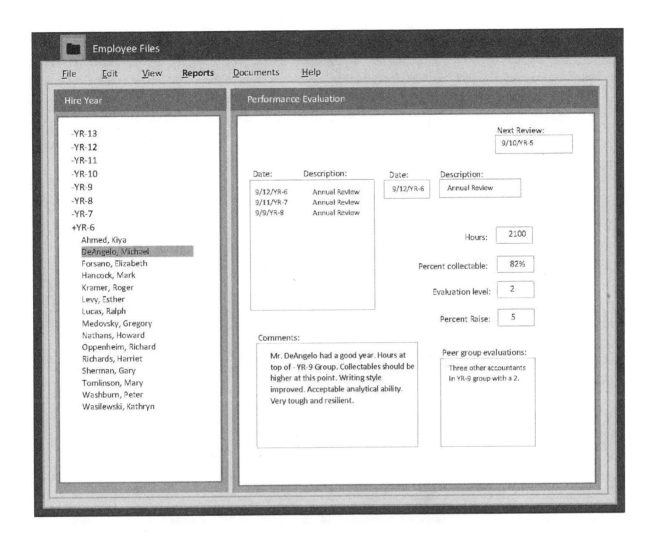

Exhibit 5D

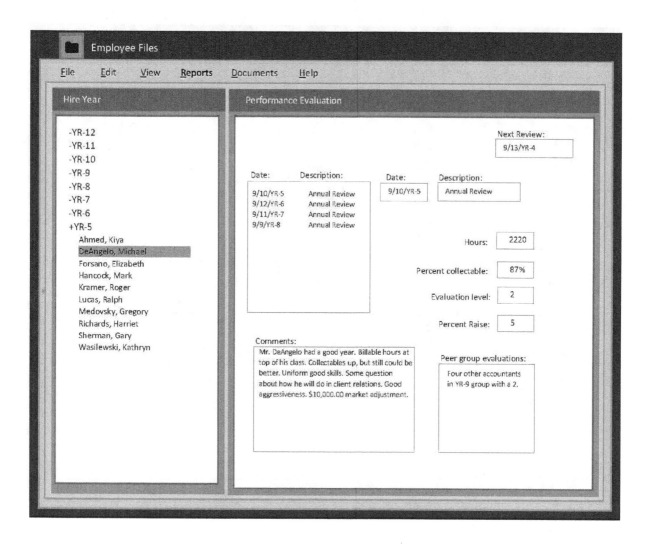

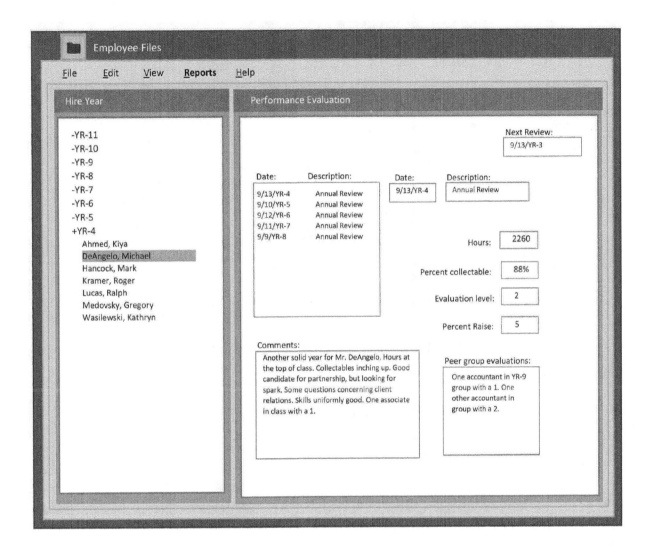

Exhibit 5F

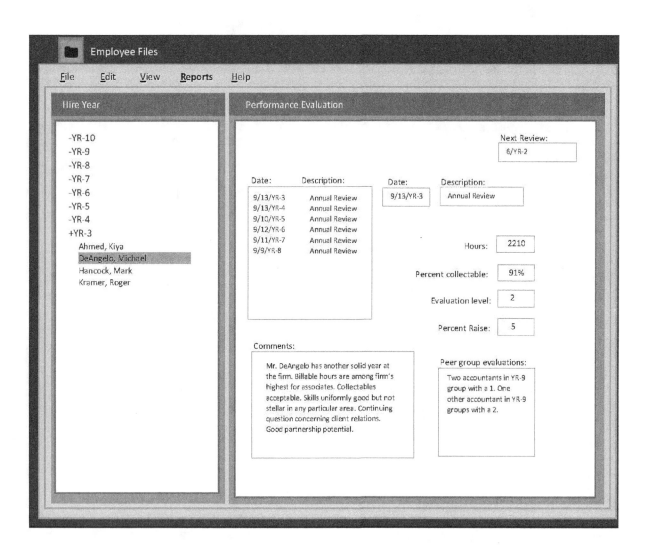

Employee Files

File   Edit   View   **Reports**   Help

Hire Year

-YR-10
-YR-9
-YR-8
-YR-7
-YR-6
-YR-5
-YR-4
+YR-3
    Ahmed, Kiya
    DeAngelo, Michael
    Hancock, Mark
    Kramer, Roger

Performance Evaluation

Next Review:
6/YR-2

Date: Description: Date: Description:
9/13/YR-3   Annual Review   9/13/YR-3   Annual Review
9/13/YR-4   Annual Review
9/10/YR-5   Annual Review
9/12/YR-6   Annual Review
9/11/YR-7   Annual Review   Hours: 2210
9/9/YR-8   Annual Review

Percent collectable: 91%

Evaluation level: 2

Percent Raise: 5

Comments:

Mr. DeAngelo has another solid year at
the firm. Billable hours are among firm's
highest for associates. Collectables
acceptable. Skills uniformly good but not
stellar in any particular area. Continuing
question concerning client relations.
Good partnership potential.

Peer group evaluations:

Two accountants in YR-9
group with a 1. One
other accountant in YR-9
groups with a 2.

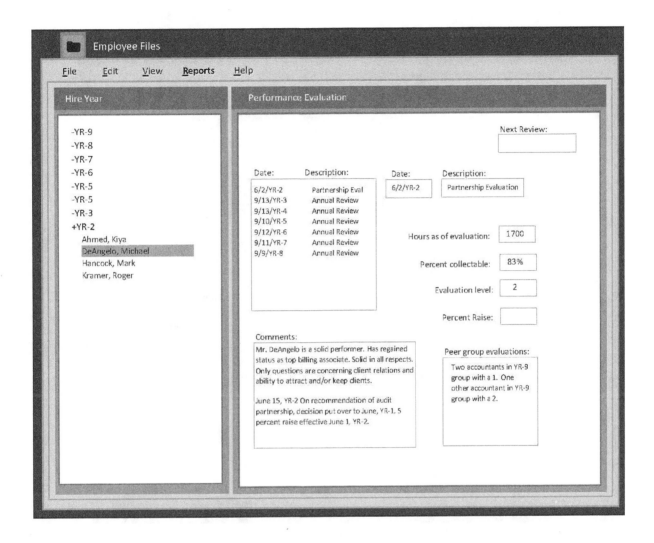

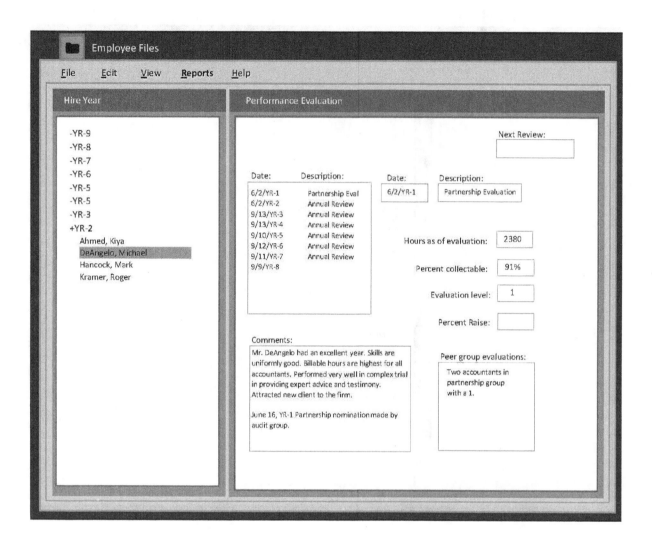

NITA COMPUTER WORLD

"A WORLD BETTER"

1550 Science Drive, Nita City, Nita 57818 ✦ 819.555.9080 ✦ NCWComputers.nita

July 8, YR-3

Mr. Paul Buckner
Cooper & Stewart
Four Independence Square
Nita City, Nita

Dear Paul:

I have just returned from a Board of Directors meeting for the company and wanted to report how pleased the board is over the outcome in our most recent litigation. You and your group's advice on theory, preparation of our lawyers for deposition, and your testimony was an integral and necessary part of our success. As you may know, several of the companies who failed to settle the case were hit pretty hard by the jury. The work of you and your team, together with your wise counsel, saved us a great deal of money.

Please pass on my thanks to your litigation support audit team. In particular, I was most impressed with the performance of your senior accountant, Kiya Ahmed. She did a fine job preparing counsel on our trade secret protective order, the positive result of which positioned us well for settlement of the case. I do not know her status at the firm, but NCW would be pleased to have her work on other matters for us in the future. Specifically, Bill Weisman is lead accountant on another lawsuit with a similar trade secrets issue, and I hope that she can be assigned to that case.

I trust that you and your team enjoyed your recent trip. I'll get a full report when we meet next week.

Warm regards,

Howard Meltzer
Vice President
General Counsel

cc: Ms. Kiya Ahmed
    Cooper & Stewart

COOPER & STEWART

Four Independence Square
Nita City, Nita 57816
819.555.3458

Compilation of employment records for staff accountants hired YR-9
while on partnership track.
Entries show name of accountant, evaluation, and billable hours for each year with
firm.

NAME	YR-8	YR-7	YR-6	YR-5	YR-4	YR-3	YR-2
Ahmed, Kiya	3 1770	2 1960	2 2020	2 2040	3 1830	1 2300	2 1750
DeAngelo, Michael	2 1880	2 1910	2 2100	2 2220	2 2260	2 2210	2 2250
Isenberg, David	4 1740	4 1800					
Forsano, Elizabeth	3 1700	3 1820	3 1860	3 1900			
Hancock, Mark	3 1750	3 1850	2 2060	2 2160	2 2210	2 2190	1 1650*
Jenner, Jennifer	4 1650	3 1820					
Kramer, Roger	2 1850	2 1900	2 1910	2 1940	1 2070	1 2050	1 1550*
Levy, Esther	3 1790	3 1840	3 1890				
Lucas, Ralph	4 1740	3 1800	3 1810	3 1890	3 1940		
Marin, John	4 1710	4 1740					
Medovsky, Gregory	4 1740	3 1810	3 1860	3 1910	3 1960		

(handwritten next to YR-2 column: 1995 1700)

Compilation of employment records—Staff Accountants hired YR-9 (continued)

NAME	YR-8	YR-7	YR-6	YR-5	YR-4	YR-3	YR-2
Nathans, Howard	3 1760	3 1800	4 1780				
Oppenheim, Richard	4 1650	3 1850	3 1950	P/A**			
Polen, Craig	3 1780	3 1880					
Richards, Harriet	3 1780	3 1840	3 1880	3 1980			
Sherman, Gary	2 1850	2 1920	3 1880	2 2010			
Tomlinson, Mary	3 1800	3 1820	3 1890	P/A**			
Washburn, Peter	3 1740	3 1880	4 1650				
Wasilewski, Kathryn	3 1780	3 1860	3 1900	3 1930	3 1960		

* Elected to partnership, June, YR-2. Hours reflect those accumulated through June 1, YR-2.

** Accepted position as permanent senior accountant with firm. No longer on partnership track.

COOPER & STEWART

Four Independence Square
Nita City, Nita 57816
819.555.3458

INCOMING PHONE MESSAGES

NAME: Paul Buckner   ASSISTANT: Mary Langford

DATE	PERSON CALLING	PHONE NUMBER	MESSAGE
7/9/YR-2	David Greenburg IRS	202-544-1770	Please call re: Tax Audit
7/9/YR-2	Bill Grayson NCW	530-1000	Please call re: Cal. litigation
7/9/YR-2	Mary Carson Nita Country Club	555-1444 member/guest	Please call re: tournament
7/9/YR-2	John Randall Morrison & Farrow	555-5880 Ahmed	Please call re: recommendation
7/9/YR-2	Amanda	Home or car	Dinner with Mitchells
7/9/YR-2	Gerry Mason Cooper & Davis	215-878-3000	Please call re: Rogers v. Preston Tools

Exhibit 9

COOPER & STEWART

Four Independence Square
Nita City, Nita 57816
819.555.3458

INCOMING PHONE MESSAGES

NAME: Paul Buckner **ASSISTANT:** Mary Langford

DATE	PERSON CALLING	PHONE NUMBER	MESSAGE
7/15/YR-2	Bill Grayson NCW	530-1000	Call re: Cal. litigation
7/15/YR-2	Harriet Miller Carter & Carroll	441-4100	Please call re: Ahmed recommendation
7/15/YR-2	Rob Bryant	x8110	Please call
7/15/YR-2	Amanda	At Club	Dinner with Meltons
7/15/YR-2	Roger Warren Melinson & Capps	487-6000	Please call re: Ahmed recommendation
7/15/YR-2	Andy Freeman Cooper & Davis	215-878-3000	Please call re: Rogers v. Preston Tools outstanding interrogatories

COOPER & STEWART

Four Independence Square
Nita City, Nita 57816
819.555.3458

*Paul
This is the
recommendation
letter. BW*

Dear

It is with great pleasure that I write you concerning Ms. Kiya Ahmed who has applied for a position with your firm. Over the past several years I have worked closely with her and feel well qualified to evaluate her abilities as an accountant working primarily in our audit group.

Ms. Ahmed came to us after a distinguished career at the University of Nita School Business School MBA Program (online program) where she graduated first in her class and received numerous awards. During her time at Cooper & Stewart she has worked on the most sophisticated of matters and has demonstrated enormous talent as an accountant working on challenging audits, some of which have required litigation support, and close working relationships with litigators.

She possesses analytical prowess, a talent for precision and persuasiveness in writing, and the ability to articulate her clients' positions to her clients. She has, quite frankly, excelled in all areas of audit accounting.

In addition to her superb skills, Ms. Ahmed has shown excellent maturity and does very well in client interaction. In fact, in a recent engagement, involving one of our most sophisticated clients, she was commended by the client, in writing, at the successful conclusion of the matter.

In closing, let me say that you will have a difficult time finding a better addition to your firm than Ms. Ahmed. If I can be of further assistance, please do not hesitate to call.

Sincerely,
Paul Buckner

COOPER & STEWART

Four Independence Square
Nita City, Nita 57816
819.555.3458

June 27, YR-2

Mr. John Randall
Morrison & Farrow
Four Courthouse Square
Nita City, Nita 57817

No further interview.
not interested. JR

Dear John,

It is with great pleasure that I write in recommendation of Ms. Kiya Ahmed for a position with your firm. Although my opportunities to work with her have been limited because of some travel restrictions she imposed, I have worked with her on several engagements which provide me with an adequate basis to evaluate her abilities.

Ms. Ahmed possesses a fine mind and generally applies it to her work. She has performed the full range of accounting duties at the firm and her work has been well received by myself and my partners. Her analytical skills are solid, and she presents her analysis in a clear writing style. In addition, while her opportunities have been limited, she has provided litigation support for accounting issues for several law firms representing our longtime clients.

In closing, let me say that a decision to hire Ms. Ahmed for a senior accounting position with your firm would be a good one. I am sure that you will be satisfied with her performance. If I can be of further assistance, please feel free to call.

Warm regards,

P.S. John -- be careful on this one. Call me.
PB

Paul Buckner

Paul Buckner
Chair, Audit Group

COOPER & STEWART

Four Independence Square
Nita City, Nita 57816
819.555.3458

July 7, YR-2

Harriet Miller
Carter & Carroll
410 Pine Street
Nita City, Nita 57816

Dear Ms. Miller,

It is with great pleasure that I write in recommendation of Ms. Kiya Ahmed for a position with your firm. Although my opportunities to work with her have been limited because of some travel restrictions she imposed, I have worked with her on several cases which provide me with an adequate basis to evaluate her abilities.

Ms. Ahmed possesses a fine mind and generally applies it to her work. She has performed the full range of accounting duties at the firm and her work has been well received by myself and my partners. Her analytical skills are solid, and she presents her analysis in a clear writing style. In addition, while her opportunities have been limited, she has provided litigation support for several law firms representing our longtime clients.

In closing, let me say that a decision to hire Ms. Ahmed for a senior accounting position with your firm would be a good one. I am sure that you will be satisfied with her performance. If I can be of further assistance, please feel free to call.

Sincerely yours,

Paul Buckner

Paul Buckner
Chair, Audit Group

COOPER & STEWART

Four Independence Square
Nita City, Nita 57816
819.555.3458

July 8, YR-2

Regina Woskinzt
Melinson & Capps
1420 JFK Boulevard
Nita City, Nita 57801

Dear Regina,

It is with great pleasure that I write in recommendation of Ms. Kiya Ahmed for a position with your firm. Although my opportunities to work with her have been limited because of some travel restrictions she imposed, I have worked with her on several cases which provide me with an adequate basis to evaluate her abilities.

Ms. Ahmed possesses a fine mind and generally applies it to her work. She has performed the full range of accounting duties at the firm and her work has been well received by myself and my partners. Her analytical skills are solid, and she presents her analysis in a clear writing style. In addition, while her opportunities have been limited, she has provided litigation support for several law firms representing our longtime clients.

In closing, let me say that a decision to hire Ms. Ahmed for a senior accounting position with your firm would be a good one. I am sure that you will be satisfied with her performance. If I can be of further assistance, please feel free to call.

Warm regards,

Paul Buckner

Paul Buckner
Chair, Audit Group

Spoke to P.B.
–Not a good
lateral candidate
R.W.

U. S. Equal Employment Opportunity Commission

EEOC FORM 131 (11/09)

Cooper & Stewart Four Independence Square Nita City, Nita 57815	**PERSON FILING CHARGE** Kiya Ahmed THIS PERSON *(check one or both)* [X] Claims To Be Aggrieved [ ] Is Filing on Behalf of Other(s) **EEOC CHARGE NO.** YR-2-49985

NOTICE OF CHARGE OF DISCRIMINATION
(See the enclosed for additional information)

This is notice that a charge of employment discrimination has been filed against your organization under:

[X] Title VII of the Civil Rights Act (Title VII)   [ ] The Equal Pay Act (EPA)   [ ] The Americans with Disabilities Act (ADA)

[ ] The Age Discrimination in Employment Act (ADEA)   [ ] The Genetic Information Nondiscrimination Act (GINA)

The boxes checked below apply to our handling of this charge:

1. [ ] No action is required by you at this time.

2. [ ] Please call the EEOC Representative listed below concerning the further handling of this charge.

3. [X] Please provide by **8/1/YR-2** a statement of your position on the issues covered by this charge, with copies of any supporting documentation to the EEOC Representative listed below. Your response will be placed in the file and considered as we investigate the charge. A prompt response to this request will make it easier to conclude our investigation.

4. [ ] Please respond fully by _____ to the enclosed request for information and send your response to the EEOC Representative listed below. Your response will be placed in the file and considered as we investigate the charge. A prompt response to this request will make it easier to conclude our investigation.

5. [ ] EEOC has a Mediation program that gives parties an opportunity to resolve the issues of a charge without extensive investigation or expenditure of resources. If you would like to participate, please say so on the enclosed form and respond by

   to

   If you DO NOT wish to try Mediation, you must respond to any request(s) made above by the date(s) specified there.

For further inquiry on this matter, please use the charge number shown above. Your position statement, your response to our request for information, or any inquiry you may have should be directed to:

Terry Mattoon
_____
EEOC Representative

Telephone   212-555-4444

Enclosure(s):   [ ] Copy of Charge

CIRCUMSTANCES OF ALLEGED DISCRIMINATION

[ ] Race [ ] Color [X] Sex [X] Religion [X] National Origin [ ] Age [ ] Disability [ ] Retaliation [ ] Genetic Information [ ] Other

Claimant states that she was denied partnership at the accounting firm of Cooper & Stewart because of her refusal to continue a sexual relationship with Paul Buckner, a partner in the accounting firm of Cooper & Stewart. She further states that the accounting firm participated in the denial of partnership on that basis. She further states that she was denied partnership because of her national origin and Muslim faith.

Date 6/30/YR-2	Name / Title of Authorized Official Terry Mattoon	Signature *Terry Mattoon*

COOPER & STEWART

Four Independence Square
Nita City, Nita 57816
819.555.3458

September 1, YR-2

Ms. Terry Mattoon
Equal Employment Opportunity Commission
22 Constitution Plaza
Nita City, Nita 57815

Dear Ms. Mattoon:

I am writing on behalf of the accounting firm of Cooper & Stewart in response to your correspondence of June 30, YR-2, in which you provided to us a Notice of Charge of Discrimination by Ms. Kiya Ahmed.

Cooper & Stewart categorically denies that the negative partnership decision by the firm concerning Ms. Ahmed was on any basis other than the merits. Ms. Ahmed was denied partnership in the firm because her billable hours were not acceptable, the quality of her work was not acceptable, her ability to attract business to the firm was not acceptable, and because in times of personal crisis she was unable to adequately perform her job functions at the firm.

If you have any further questions concerning this unfounded allegation, please feel free to contact me.

Sincerely,

Robert Bryant

Robert Bryant
Chair, Cooper & Stewart

Exhibit 16

EEOC Form 161-B (10/96)

U.S. EQUAL EMPLOYMENT OPPORTUNITY COMMISSION

NOTICE OF RIGHT TO SUE (*ISSUED ON REQUEST*)

To:	From:
Ms. Kiya Ahmed 7010 Greenhill Road Nita City, Nita 57820	Equal Employment Opportunity Commission 22 Constitution Plaza Nita City, Nita 57816

☐ On behalf of person(s) aggrieved whose identity is CONFIDENTIAL (29 CFR § 1601.7(a))

Charge No.	EEOC Representative	Telephone No.
YR-2-49985	Terry Mattoon	819-555-4444

(See also the additional information attached to this form.)

NOTICE TO THE PERSON AGGRIEVED :

Title VII of the Civil Rights Act of 1964 and/or the Americans with Disabilities Act (ADA): This is your Notice of Right to Sue, issued under Title VII and/or the ADA based on the above-numbered charge. It has been issued at your request. Your lawsuit under Title VII or the ADA **must be filed in federal or state court WITHIN 90 DAYS** of your receipt of this Notice. Otherwise, your right to sue based on this charge will be lost. (The time limit for filing suit based on a state claim may be different.)

☒ More than 180 days have passed since the filing of this charge.

☐ Less than 180 days have passed since the filing of this charge, but I have determined that it is unlikely that the EEOC will be able to complete its administrative processing within 180 days from the filing of the charge.

☒ The EEOC is terminating its processing of this charge.

☐ The EEOC will continue to process this charge.

Age Discrimination in Employment Act (ADEA): You may sue under the ADEA at any time from 60 days after the charge was filed until 90 days after you receive notice that we have completed action on the charge. In this regard, **the paragraph marked below applies to your case:**

☐ The EEOC is closing your case. Therefore, your lawsuit under the ADEA **must be filed in federal or state court WITHIN 90 DAYS of your receipt of this Notice.** Otherwise, your right to sue based on the above-numbered charge will be lost.

☐ The EEOC is continuing its handling of your ADEA case. However, if 60 days have passed since the filing of your charge, you may file suit in federal or state court under the ADEA at this time.

Equal Pay Act (EPA): You already have the right to sue under the EPA (filing an EEOC charge is not required.) EPA suits must be brought in federal or state court within 2 years (3 years for willful violations) of the alleged EPA underpayment. This means that **backpay due for any violations that occurred more than 2 years (3 years)** before you file suit may not be collectible.

If you file suit based on this charge, please send a copy of your court complaint to this office.

On behalf of the Commission

Terry Mattoon
_____
Terry Mattoon

12/28/YR-2
_____
(Date Mailed)

Enclosure(s)
   Information sheet
   Copy of Charge

cc: Respondents

COOPER & STEWART

Four Independence Square
Nita City, Nita 57816
819.555.3458

October 15, YR-2

Dean Martin Purcell
University of Nita School of Law
One Campus Center
Nita City, Nita 57825

Dear Marty,

It is with great pleasure that I write you concerning Ms. Kiya Ahmed, who has applied for a teaching position at the law school as a Practice Professor. Over the past several years I have worked closely with her and feel well qualified to evaluate her abilities as an accountant, especially in litigation support, which I believe should translate over into the classroom. And, of course, I believe it wise that your students understand the basics of audit as well as tax accounting to prepare themselves for modern litigation practice.

Ms. Ahmed came to us after a distinguished career in the Business School, where, as I am sure you have found out, she was first in her online MBA class, which I can guarantee is every bit as challenging as the regular MBA program. During her time at Cooper & Stewart, she has worked on the most sophisticated of matters and has demonstrated enormous talent.

She possesses analytical prowess, a talent for precision and persuasiveness in writing, and the ability to articulate her analysis in a consumable form for lawyers involved in complex civil matters.

In addition to her superb skills, Ms. Ahmed has shown excellent maturity and does very well in client interaction. In fact, in a recent case, involving one of our most sophisticated clients, she was commended by the client, in writing, at the successful conclusion of the case.

In closing, let me say that you will have a difficult time finding a better addition to your faculty than Ms. Ahmed. If I can be of any further assistance, please do not hesitate to call.

Please give my best to Ellen and the children.

Warm Regards,

Paul Buckner

Paul Buckner

Exhibit 18

AFFIDAVIT OF JOHN RANDALL

My name is John Randall. Until recently I was a partner in the firm of Morrison & Farrow in Nita City. I have retired from the practice of accounting as of November 1, YR-1 and will be moving to France next month. I do not anticipate returning to the United States soon.

I have agreed to give this affidavit before this court reporter and counsel for both the plaintiff and defendants in the case of Ahmed v. Cooper & Stewart, et al. in order to tell what I know about the facts of this case.

In the summer of YR-2 I received an impressive resume from an accountant at Cooper & Stewart by the name of Kiya Ahmed. I no longer have that resume but the document shown to me marked as Exhibit 1 looks familiar—although there were obviously no job entries beyond her position at Cooper & Stewart. The resume also listed Paul Buckner at C&S as a reference.

I have known Paul for over twenty years. I respect his opinion on accounting talent, so I asked Ms. Ahmed to have Paul send me a letter of recommendation. Shortly thereafter I received his letter of recommendation. Although the letter was not negative, I wouldn't call it a positive letter either. His evaluation of Ms. Ahmed was lukewarm. In addition, he included a handwritten note that I should take care regarding this candidate or something to that effect. Looking at what's been marked as Exhibit 11, that is the letter I received. The second handwritten note on the letter is in my handwriting.

When I received Paul's letter, I gave him a call and asked for an oral evaluation. He told me that Ms. Ahmed had been turned down for partnership, a fact that I had assumed given her years at the firm, and the fact that she was applying for a job with us. He also told me that Ms. Ahmed was not a good candidate for my practice, which was litigation support for complex commercial and tax white-collar-criminal practice, because there was reason to question her toughness and ability to cope with the stress inherent in my kind of practice. I asked him whether she would be suitable for the group at the firm that handled civil litigation in similar financial matters where an opening had just occurred. He told me that in his opinion Ms. Ahmed was not cut out for litigation support of any sort, that she was just not reliable.

As a result of the letter and the phone call, I did not pursue hiring Ms. Ahmed, nor did I refer her resume to the civil side of Morrison and Farrow.

Given her resume, absent the information from Paul Buckner and my interview of her, we certainly would have considered Ms. Ahmed for a position with our firm, on either the civil or criminal side. She seemed well qualified, at least on paper. Whether we would have hired her is an open question; it would have depended on her performance in the full interview with numerous partners and junior accountants and whether we thought she would fit into the firm. Unlike C&S, we were then and are now a medium-sized accounting firm, so personality conflicts are a greater problem for us, and so the interview and our evaluation of how Ms. Ahmed would fit in with the other men and women at the firm would have been an important consideration. Although my initial meeting was positive, after Paul's letter, we decided not to take her to the formal interview process and declined her application.

Further the affiant sayeth not.

John Randall

John Randall

Subscribed and sworn before me this 9th day of October, YR-1.

Mary Williams

Mary Williams
Notary Public

JURY INSTRUCTIONS

1. The court will now instruct you as to the claims and defenses of each party and the law governing the case. Please pay close attention to these instructions. You must arrive at your verdict by applying the law as you are now instructed to the facts as you find them.

2. The parties to this case are Ms. Ahmed, the plaintiff, and Mr. Buckner and the accounting firm of C&S, the co-defendants. Ms. Ahmed has sued Mr. Buckner and the accounting firm, seeking to recover damages based on a number of claims.

a. First, Ms. Ahmed claims that Mr. Buckner and the firm discriminated against her on the basis of her gender in violation of Title VII of the Civil Rights Act.

On this gender discrimination claim, the plaintiff, Ms. Ahmed, has the burden of proving, by a preponderance of the evidence, a prima facie case of discrimination. To do so, she must show: 1) she belongs to a protected class, i.e. she is a female; 2) she applied for a position with her employer (in this case, partnership in the accounting firm of C&S) which was available and for which she was qualified; 3) despite her qualifications, she was rejected for the position; and 4) after her rejection, the position remained open and her employer sought male applicants of plaintiff's qualifications.

If Ms. Ahmed succeeds in proving the prima facie case of gender discrimination, the burden shifts to the defendant(s) to articulate some legitimate, non-discriminatory reason for Ms. Ahmed's rejection.

Should the defendant(s) meet the burden of articulating a legitimate, non-discriminatory reason for rejecting Ms. Ahmed for partnership in the accounting firm, the plaintiff, Ms. Ahmed, must, then, prove, by a preponderance of the evidence, that the reasons offered by the defendant(s) were not the true reasons for her rejection, but rather a pretext for discrimination.

b. Second, the plaintiff, Ms. Ahmed, claims that the defendants, Mr. Buckner and the accounting firm of C&S, committed the act of Quid Pro Quo Gender Discrimination in violation of Title VII of the Civil Rights Act.

In order to prevail on this claim, the Plaintiff, Ms. Ahmed, must prove, by a preponderance of the evidence, that: 1) she was an employee of the defendant(s) and a female, 2) she was subjected to unwelcome sexual harassment in the form of sexual advances or requests for sexual favors, 3) the harassment complained of was based on sex, and 4) her submission to the unwelcomed advances was an express or implied condition for receiving job benefits or that her refusal to submit to a supervisor's sexual demands resulted in tangible job detriment.

Or Ms. Ahmed must prove by a preponderance of the evidence, that 1) she was an employee of the defendant and a female, 2) that she ended a voluntary sexual relationship with the defendant Buckner, and 3) that in retaliation of her actions the defendant C&S denied her a partnership in the firm and terminated her as an employee of the firm.

c. Third, the plaintiff, Ms. Ahmed, claims that the defendant(s), Mr. Buckner and the firm of C&S, committed the act of gender discrimination by creating a "hostile working environment," in violation of Title VII of the Civil Rights Act.

In order to prevail on this "hostile working environment" claim, the plaintiff, Ms. Ahmed, must prove: 1) she was an employee and a member of a protected class, i.e., a female; 2) she was subjected to unwelcome sexual harassment; 3) the harassment complained of was based on sex; and 4) the harassment complained of affected a "term, condition or privilege" of employment in that it was sufficiently severe or pervasive to alter the condition of Ms. Ahmed's employment and create an abusive working environment.

d. Fourth, Ms. Ahmed claims that Mr. Buckner and the firm discriminated against her on the basis of her national origin and religion in violation of Title VII of the Civil Rights Act.

On this discrimination claim, the plaintiff, Ms. Ahmed, has the burden of proving, by a preponderance of the evidence, a prima facie case of discrimination. To do so, she must show: 1) she belongs to a protected class, i.e., she is an Egyptian/Muslim; 2) she applied for a position with her employer (in this case, partnership in the accounting firm of C&S) which was available and for which she was qualified; 3) despite her qualifications, she was rejected for the position; and 4) after her rejection, the position remained open and her employer sought male applicants of plaintiff's qualifications.

If Ms. Ahmed succeeds in proving the prima facie case of national origin and religious discrimination, the burden shifts to the defendant(s) to articulate some legitimate, non-discriminatory reason for Ms. Ahmed's rejection.

Should the defendant(s) meet the burden of articulating a legitimate, non-discriminatory reason for rejecting Ms. Ahmed for partnership in the accounting firm, the plaintiff, Ms. Ahmed, must, then, prove, by a preponderance of the evidence, that the reasons offered by the defendant(s) were not the true reasons for her rejection, but rather a pretext for discrimination.

If you find that Ms. Ahmed has proved any or all of the above claims, you may award damages as follows:

> 1) Award Ms. Ahmed the amount of money in wages and fringe benefits which you determine Ms. Ahmed lost as a result of defendant(s)' unlawful conduct from the date of her termination from C&S to the present with interest at the statutory rate, and

> 2) Reinstate Ms. Ahmed as a partner in the firm of C&S, or, in the alternative, award her "front pay" in the amount of wages and benefits which Ms. Ahmed will lose in the future because of her unlawful termination from C&S.

If you find that Ms. Ahmed has proved none of the gender discrimination claims, you will render a verdict for the defendant(s) and award no damages.

3. In addition to the above-mentioned claims of gender discrimination, Ms. Ahmed also has sued the defendant(s), Buckner and C&S, seeking to recover damages for the tort of defamation.

In order to prevail on her claim of defamation, the plaintiff, Ms. Ahmed, must prove, by a preponderance of the evidence, that the defendant(s) published at least one statement which defamed her, causing her harm.

"Publication" means that the defendant(s) communicated by speaking or writing an idea to some other person.

A communication is "defamatory" if, taken as a whole, it tends to harm the reputation of the victim as to lower her in the estimation of the community or to deter a third party from associating or dealing with her.

If you find that the communication, even if it was defamatory of the plaintiff, was substantially true, you will return a verdict in favor of the defendant(s) and against the plaintiff.

If you find that the defendant(s)' communication was defamatory, but was made subject to a conditional privilege, then you must find for the defendant(s) unless the plaintiff proves that the privilege was abused by the defendant(s) in that they acted knowingly, recklessly, or maliciously.

In this case, I find and instruct you a conditional privilege applies. This privilege conditionally protects statements made where the publisher(s) of the statement (the defendant(s)) reasonably believe(s) that he or she is protecting the interest of the recipient of the statement or a person who may act on the defamatory statement. For example, the conditional statement extends to statements of reference made by an employer about a present or past employee to a prospective employer. Thus, the references provided by Buckner to Ahmed's prospective employers are within the protection of the conditional privilege.

However, you shall find that the defendant(s) lost the protection of the privilege if the plaintiff proves, by a preponderance of the evidence, that the defendant(s) defamed her with knowledge of its falsity, recklessly (that is, without regard to whether it was true or false), or intentionally.

If you find that the defendant(s) are liable for defamation, the plaintiff is entitled to be fairly and adequately compensated for all harm she suffered as a result of the defamatory communications published by the defendant(s). The injuries for which you may compensate the plaintiff by an award of damages against the defendant(s) include:

> 1) the actual harm to the plaintiff's reputation which you find resulted from the defendant(s) conduct, and

> 2) the emotional distress, mental anguish, and humiliation which you find the plaintiff suffered as a result of the defendant(s)' conduct (as well as the bodily harm which you find was caused by such suffering).

Special Instruction on Agency

A principal is liable for the acts of its agent if the agent is liable, where: 1) a principal-agent relationship exists, and 2) the agent performs the acts for which he is liable while acting within the scope of his employment and in furtherance of the principal's business. I instruct you that defendant Ahmed was, at all times material to this lawsuit, the agent of the defendant C&S, and was at all times acting within the scope of her employment with C&S. Thus, all conduct performed by Buckner is the responsibility not only of him, but of C&S.

IN THE UNITED STATES
DISTRICT COURT
DISTRICT OF NITA

KIYA AHMED,   )
Plaintiff,   )   CIVIL ACTION NO. YR-1-4678
)
v.   )   JURY TRIAL DEMANDED
)
PAUL BUCKNER   )
and   )
COOPER & STEWART,   )
Defendants.   )

We, the jury, and each of us, finds:

1.   __(a) On Claim 2a, for the Plaintiff in the amount of $ _____

        __(b) On Claim 2a, for the Defendant(s).

(Answer either Question l(a) or l(b) .)

2.   __(a) On Claim 2b, for the Plaintiff in the amount of $ _____

        __(b) On Claim 2b, for the Defendant(s)

(Answer either Question 2(a) or 2(b) .)

3.   __(a) On Claim 2c, for the Plaintiff in the amount of $ _____

        __(b) On Claim 2c, for the Defendants.

(Answer either Question 3(a) or 3(b) .)

4.   __(a) On Claim 2d, for the Plaintiff in the amount of $ _____

        __(b) On Claim 2d, for the Defendants.

(Answer either Question 4(a) or 4(b) .)

5.	__(a) On Claim 3, for the Plaintiff in the amount of $ _____

	__(b) On Claim 3, for the Defendants.

(Answer either Question 5(a) or 5(b) .)

_____

Foreperson